# Where Do I Know You From...

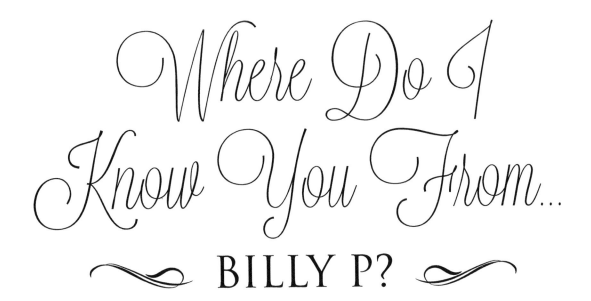

# Where Do I Know You From...

## ~ BILLY P? ~

A  P E R S O N A L  M E M O I R E

**Made for Grace**
**PUBLISHING**

# PRAISE FOR
# WHO IS THIS BILLY P. GUY?

The story of Billy P. strikes a familiar note with those of us who were raised in post WW2 America. He's the boy next door, the son you'd love to call your own, the all-American kid who grows up to live his dream - serving his country, marrying his college sweetheart, and raising a family. His life, like all of our lives, has it highs and lows, joys and sorrows. It's a life worth living, and a life worth reading about.

*~Cheryl Kuhn*

Thanks for taking me along on your journey! I felt like I was a part of all the happenings! Loved the honeymoon.

*~ Marlene Snyder*

Bill has given such a gift for his family to cherish and pass down for generations to come.

*~Greg Leff*

Wonderful family story, written from the heart. Enjoyed every minute. Fun to read family stories. Love the author, and fun, entertaining stories.

*~ Melody Walsh.*

We all have a special story to tell. It's ours alone to share. One's memories are ways to say "We Have Lived" and connect our humanity with the rest of the world.

*~Phyllis Brouard.*

Bill's writing made me feel like he was sitting in front of me reading his stories. What a blessing.

*~Barbara Grimes.*

Hearing a story told by Bill Perry is like going on an adventure. Especially if it's about his life, which 90% of the time includes his wife Phyllis. Bill will say his memory isn't as good as it used to be, which he has been saying since he was 23 years old. Don't believe it! Bill not only remembers his stories, but he tells them in "technicolor," with not a detail left out. An easy read, yes, but just as captivating as if you'd heard them told by Bill himself, with Phyllis close by interjecting with her sweet laughter as if she'd heard the story for the first time. Stories like these should be put into a book.

*~ Loretta Sassaman , Spin That 45 / Freelance Writer / Music Reviewer*

Made For Grace Publishing
P.O. Box 1775 Issaquah, WA 98027
**www.MadeForGrace.com**

Copyright © 2015 Bill Perry

Distributed by Made For Grace Publishing
Cover Design by DeeDee Heathman
Interior Design by DeeDee Heathman

**Library of Congress Cataloging-in-Publication data**

Perry, Bill
    Where Do I Know You From Billy P?: A Personal Memoire. Book 1
        p. cm.
        ISBN: 9781613398012
        LCCN: 2015907871
    1.   Personal Memoirs  2.  Motivational & Inspirational

For further information contact Made For Grace Publishing +14255266480 or email **service@madeforsuccess.net**

Printed in the United States of America

# TABLE OF CONTENTS

## WHERE DO I KNOW YOU FROM BILLY P?

## *** *To Phyllis, My Wife* ***

Wolkramshausen
17. Maerz
5. Mai
ex decreto
25. Februar

# INTRODUCTION

## WHO IS THIS BILLY P. GUY?

M y creative writing friend and mentor recently asked me a question I had no answer for. The question seemed simple. How would I describe myself to someone I have never met face to face, yet they ask the same question that so many people have in recent years: "Where do I know you from?" At first the answer seemed quite simple and then I got to thinking about it and soon it was more difficult than I had ever imagined.

I would describe myself as a very "liquid" person, starting with wetting the bed until I was ten. I've been told that I'm very emotional and have tear ducts that are always ready to explode when I'm talking or writing about my family.

I've been called so many different names in the years gone by: "Blimp," "Pear-Shaped," Bed Wetter," and more recently the "Guy2go2" the "Just Putt'n Around Guy" and "There's Trouble." I've learned to "roll with the punches" to "suck it up" and I have the amazing ability to "start all over again". One thing I have never been called is a "Loser" and I wouldn't have it any other way.

I truly believe that I have been blessed by the Lord who has given me the ability to express myself by using my thoughts and fingers in a manner that may help you have a few laughs and maybe a tear or two. The book does not come with Kleenex.

Who is this Billy P. guy?
He's someone you met by chance
and we're glad you asked the question,

"Where DO I know you from!?"

Wolkramshausen

17. März 183.
5. Mai

... von Wermb'schen Güter abgeschrieben ...

... ca decreto vom 25. Februar 1831 ...

# CHAPTER 1

## WHY ME? WHY NOT?

*T*here must be a reason for writing this book which I call *Where Do I Know You From…Billy P?*

It must be from wanting to leave something behind for my wife, Phyllis, our children, grandchildren and great grandchildren, and all our great friends we have come to know and love over the years.

I struggled for almost three years trying to find a job. My friends kept asking me how I was doing and what was I working on. There really wasn't an answer and I got tired of making up stuff.

I decided to stick with just one story and told the same story over and over which solved my problem, and to my amazement, my friends were all impressed and asked more questions.

I simply told them I was writing my life story to pass on to my family. They were amazed and so was I. Everyone said, "I wish someone had done that for me so I could remember my family's history."

In their minds, I instantly became a writer and I had no idea what I was doing. My friends were happy, I was happy, and it was great.

I can't remember the last time I had a problem standing up in front of people and bringing life to the stories I was telling. If I can bring that same life to the stories I write, there may be a future in this business.

I hope you will find my stories coming to life as you enjoy the book.

The book opens with the first day I met my future wife, Phyllis, at college, September 10th, 1963. I am so glad we met that day. If we hadn't, I might still be in a corner somewhere and never have met the hundreds of people I have had the honor of meeting through the years.

Do you like the stories that begin with
"Once upon a time?"
That's where I started and now
the 1st book is yours to enjoy!

…a, meine Wohl, fla…
…n bestehen…
…, R… Jul… …emann,
…gewöhnlich… …Wolkramshausen
17. März 183… …schreiben. Fünfzig Thaler
5. Mai 183…
…nt, weil… …Bücher Hälfte, welchen solche
…ven Herr… von Wermbscher Güter abgeschrieben
…n, ex decreto vom 25. Februar 1834 … …
…zugeschrieben.

# Chapter 2

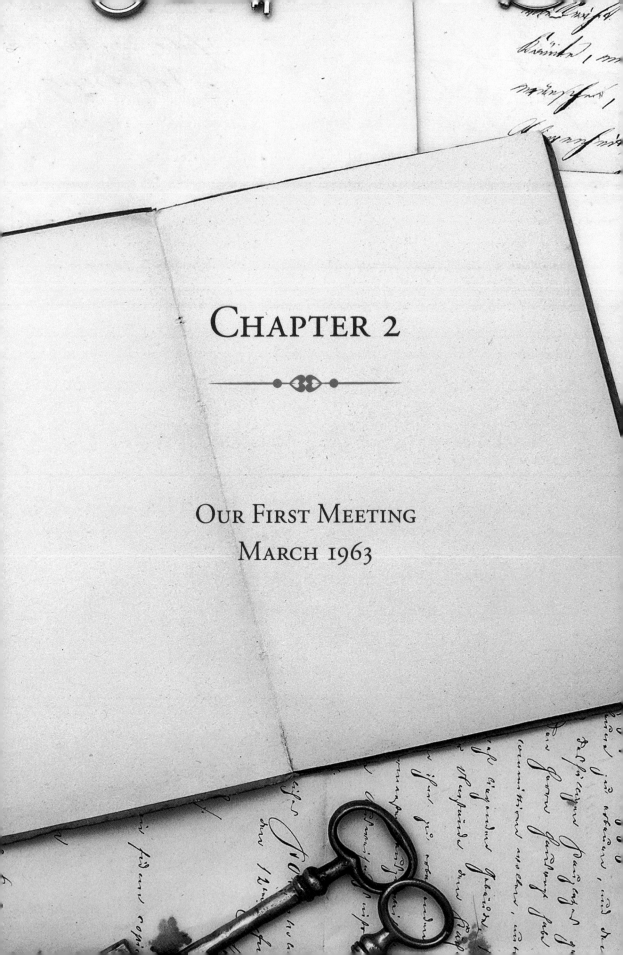

Our First Meeting

March 1963

*I* can still remember it as if it was yesterday. I was in junior college on my third try to get an AA degree. I was sitting on a cement wall waiting for the rest of the cheerleading gang to show up for practice. That may have been one of the reasons I was on my third try. Standing in front of a football crowd yelling was easy for me and sitting in a classroom was not.

Two good-looking girls walked my way, one leading and the other trailing behind. The lead girl, who was very outgoing, walked up to me and asked if I was Bill Perry. After checking my wallet briefly, I said yes. Before I could ask their names, she proceeded to introduce me to my future wife, Phyllis Brouard.

I had never seen Phyllis around the campus which was obviously a big mistake I had made. This was way back in 1963 and my memory hasn't gotten any better.

Things started off well and we began dating shortly after we met. I think it was the same night. It must have been some kind of hot romance because I was a cheerleader, she was a great looking young woman and I was in a fraternity.

Our romance continued to grow and we were engaged in September 1963. My, how time flies when you're in love.

As I mentioned before, I was in school on my third try to get my AA Degree which meant that I still had to serve my time in the armed forces which was mandatory when you turned eighteen... and there I was at twenty-two.

I took a look at all the options I had which were few and far between. I even looked at what was worn by the guys in uniform. After doing some research on the colors of the military uniforms, I remembered that my eyes were blue and that sealed the deal. I went to the Air Force recruiting office to check it out.

Before I did though, Phyllis and I had put together a plan that we were sure would be great when I got out of the Air Force in four years. It was quite simple. Phyllis had just gone to work for a company doing a job called Keypunch where she entered data into a machine that would send it on to many companies around the country including the stock market. It was the beginning of the computer age and we could have ended up at the head of the line.

My part, which the recruiter assured me I had the skills to do, would put me in the front of the line for training in this new industry.

I signed on the dotted line in February 1964 and was off to San Antonio, Texas, to Lackland Air Force Base for my basic training and then on to tech school.

Since we were going to be apart for some time, Phyllis and I decided to set the date for our wedding for after I finished basic training and tech school. The date was set for September 12th, 1964 and I can still remember that our favorite song was The Twelfth of Never.

Reality soon set in as I was off to basic training in Texas. I arrived on the military bus from the airport and this really big guy got on, assured us we were at the right place and that we should get our butts off the bus. I never saw the sign that said "Welcome to Your Future".

I never thought that being older than the kids on the bus would be a good thing, but it was. The really tall guy was our TI (training instructor) for the next six weeks. The first thing he wanted to know was who was the oldest guy in our barracks. With everyone else being eighteen to twenty, this twenty-three-year-old guy instantly became the barracks chief and second in command to help the TI. Wow, I'd been on base for less than an hour and I'd just got my first promotion. What a guy!

Boot camp was many hours of physical and mental training, getting in shape for what was to come. We learned how to take orders and follow through to the best of our ability. The toughest part for me was the push-ups, the sit-ups and running around the training field. I did have one advantage in my new position; I got to watch the others when the TI had other things to do.

When we weren't getting in shape, we were taking all types of tests to determine what we would be doing for the next four years. On one cold and dark morning around 4am, everyone had to get up, get dressed and marched off to take another battery of tests. I guess they wanted to see if our minds would work in the middle of the night. To this day I have no idea what kind of test we took.

Several weeks of training went by and then we were told that the time had come to meet with the job placement staff and be told what we would be doing for the next four years.

Of course, I was excited to get to this point and finally find out what technical school I would be attending to launch my career into the new computer world that I had been promised.

The building we were taken to was the size of two football fields, and wide open so you could see hundreds of new recruits at the same time. As our entire barracks of fifty recruits entered the building, our TI decided that he would go with me through this process since I had done a great job helping him.

My time came to find out and I could hardly wait to hear the good news. The job placement person, hereafter will be called just the JPP, spoke slowly and informed me that I had three choices; air police, cook or air traffic controller, whatever that was.

I couldn't believe what he said. What happened to the computer job that had been promised by my recruiter? Some mistake must have been made. I was then asked if I remembered the tests that I took early one morning several weeks ago. I said I remembered taking them. He then told me I hadn't passed the tests high enough to be put into that program and a choice had to be made from the options that were given. I was stunned and silent when I had to come up with an answer.

At that point, my TI spoke up for me and the job I had been doing. He suggested that maybe I could be enrolled in the air traffic school in Mississippi.

The JPP looked directly at me, then at my TI and said, "He's overweight and he couldn't pass the flying physical anyway." As I sat there, crushed by his comments, my TI spoke up again and asked why I couldn't try to lose the weight since the physicals weren't for two weeks.

The JPP seemed to chuckle under his breath and agreed that I could give it a try, and gave me an appointment for a physical in two weeks.

My TI thanked him and we got up and left the huge building with a new opportunity. I got outside, took a very deep breath and asked the TI what the heck an air traffic controller was. He chuckled when he told me that it's one of those guys who work in the control tower at airports. He also told me he would help me get in shape and lose the weight to pass the physical. I had to ask myself, "Who is this TI, anyway?"

It didn't take me long to jump on a diet and get in better shape than I was in when I walked into that football field building where hundreds of JPPs made decisions on where my life was going.

The two weeks flew by and my excess flab rolled off my body. I had done the work and was ready to pass my flying physical.

The memories of the physical have left me since it was way back in 1964. The important thing was that I passed with flying colors and new orders were cut to send me off to Biloxi, Mississippi, to air traffic control school.

My plans to be in on the ground floor of something they called the "computer business" faded quickly as I climbed on the bus for Mississippi, and the bright future that was opening up to the Perrys and their pending wedding date of September 12th, 1964.

The bus trip from San Antonio to Mississippi was over 600 miles and would take almost nine hours if we never stopped. It was finally a time that I could sit back, relax and enjoy doing absolutely nothing except think about my upcoming marriage when I got home from air traffic control school.

It was a long and uneventful ride through Texas. When we crossed the state line into great State of Mississippi, things were about to change. Once again it was time to get off the bus, stretch our legs and take care of the necessary things that had to be done.

The gas station was old, rundown and looked like no one really cared about it. As usual, we raced to the bathroom because there were none on the bus. Waiting in line is not something I do well and I decided to get a drink of water. I saw two drinking fountains across the parking lot and hurried over to quench my thirst. I was shocked to see one fountain looked great, and the other had an old sign hanging on it which read "Negro Drinking Fountain". I had never seen anything like that in my entire life and I was speechless.

I stood there for a few moments while I collected my thoughts and then asked another bus passenger why the sign was there. He quietly answered, "Look around. We're in Mississippi now and that's the way it is in the deep south."

Yes, we had crossed the Mississippi River into a world that would take some getting used to. The next forty miles to Keesler AFB passed quickly as I closed my eyes and continued to think about what I had just seen.

When I woke up we were at the gate of Keesler AFB, the Air Force's training school for future air traffic controllers. I had no idea what I would be learning and how difficult it would be. What I did know was that it wasn't air police or cook school and that was great with me.

Soon after we arrived we were informed that there would be a two week delay in the new class starting and we would be assigned duties to fill in the time. That sounded alright, until we were told that we would be working in the kitchen doing whatever the chief cook wanted.

It was just what I didn't want to hear, especially since Phyllis had set the wedding date for September 12th.

It didn't take much time for me to suck it up and get on with the kitchen delay. It was only going to be two weeks and I could handle anything so I would be back in California for the wedding.

Two weeks later, at the crack of dawn, I was shaved, showered, dressed and ready to take on this new world as an air traffic controller.

"Cleared to land"... I hoped!

It didn't take me long to ask myself the big question: "What have I've gotten myself into with this air traffic control thing?"

I was told that to graduate from this training, I would have to be able to talk to the Air Force pilots and tell them what to do and when to do it, plus know everything about the airport I was working at. I would be the "big guy in charge".

"Time out. Time out," I said. "I'm only twenty-three, still wet behind the ears and I'm getting married in California on September 12th. Isn't that enough pressure? I may have a heart attack before this is over and my future wife Phyllis would NOT be happy!"

For some reason all of my verbal efforts seemed to mean nothing to my instructors and it even encouraged them to call on me first.

When you were going through college, were you ever told that to graduate with a degree in your given profession you would have to be an expert in what you were doing?

Those were some of the first words we heard when we entered the air traffic controller program at Keesler AFB.

I had never heard those words from anyone before and at the age of twenty-three I sure didn't feel qualified to meet the lofty goals that were being set for us so soon after coming into the Air Force.

The one goal I was preparing myself for was the wedding that was being planned in California and I had to pass those classes and get home on time.

The first class I attended was a group of twenty airmen, all with the same rank which was "Airman-Zero", as I liked to call it. There was only one way to go and that was up, unless you could not handle the intensity of what went on in the control tower. Several of the young men did not do well and were reassigned to other jobs with less pressure. I soon realized that this air traffic controller job was going to be a big deal and a great opportunity for the future. Little did I know what it would take to be fully qualified and sit way up there in the control tower with so much responsibility for the lives of so many.

Our class was split in to two groups: tower controllers and radar controllers. I figured I was one of the lucky ones who could work in the control tower and see the airplanes take off and land. I always liked that when I was a civilian and Phyllis and I went to the airport to watch the planes take off, and smooch.

The training schedule was non-stop and meant to be that way. I had to learn to work with other controllers in the tower and it had to be done without mistakes. Sometimes in the classroom mistakes were made and understood. In real life, there just wouldn't be time to correct mistakes or get a do-over.

One of the realities that we learned from the beginning was that every conversation between the controllers and the pilots was recorded and saved for future review if an accident happened while you were on duty.

Every day of the three-month training program turned into a new learning experience while we learned the words and phrases we would use when we were talking with the pilots and ground crews.

We were tested and tested again to make sure we got it right, and if we didn't, we would do it again.

Near the end of our training we were finally allowed to leave the base and spend some time enjoying Biloxi and the Gold Coast. Crawfish and beer made a great combination when you didn't have a microphone to speak into.

The time passed quickly. My brain was overflowing with information and the dos and don'ts of the future.

It was time to get out into the real world to our new assignment, wherever that may be. Somewhere way back in my memory, I remember being asked where I would like to be stationed on my first assignment. For some reason I said France, Germany or someplace in Europe, and I was serious.

To the Air Force, it must have been a joke, so they sent me to the great State of Alaska, to Eielson Air Force Base outside of Fairbanks. I couldn't believe what they had done and neither could Phyllis when I told her.

Fortunately for me, Phyllis was coming to the end of all the wedding preparations and all she seemed to care about was me getting home in time for the wedding.

I'm happy to report that I made it one week before the big day with a duffle bag of winter gear for Alaska and a thirty day leave to spend with my wife-to-be.

*Our first meeting in college*
*has turned into 50 plus years*
*filled with love and compassion*
*for each other.*

Wolkramshausen
5. mai
ex decreto
25. Februar 1831

# CHAPTER 3

BRING ON THE FUTURE
OUR WEDDING AND HONEYMOON

ortunately for me, Phyllis, with help from her mom, Sadie, and best friend, Virginia, had planned a huge wedding with all the horns and whistles. The flowers had been ordered and even the reception was planned for the church gymnasium.

We were to be married in the First Baptist Church in South Gate, California. We were married by a long time friend of our families, Dr. Paul Kopp. Besides our friends and close relatives, our parents invited the entire church of 400 members.

All I had to do was round up the guys in the wedding and find a tux shop. Going to the tux shop turned into a big event. One of my good friends Dan was part of the wedding and had an Uncle Max who owned a tux shop where we could rent our tuxes at a cheap price. Uncle Max had some great ideas that he wanted to share with us. Just getting a regular tux was not in his plan. When we walked out of the shop, we all had black tuxedos with tails, white gloves, top hats and black canes. We looked like we had just stepped out of a movie production in Hollywood.

The entire wedding went off without a hitch, except for one small problem. All of the groomsmen were standing behind the stage door with me, as we were told to do. When I was given the signal by the preacher, I was told to open the door slowly and come out onto the stage as the bridesmaids and bride started walking down the center aisle in the church. My brain was racing at this point and I wanted to get started. My best man and good friend, Gordon, was standing behind me giving me encouragement when the signal came to come through the door. As I opened the door and began to step through it, Gordon whispered in my ear, "Your fly is open!"

What was I to do? I couldn't look down or try to fix my zipper. What would all 400 people in the church think I was doing?

So, I did what I had to do. I stood there smiling from ear to ear and watched my beautiful wife-to-be, walk down the aisle as everyone stood up to welcome her.

As she approached the front of the church, I stepped off the stage to meet her and her dad, Don, who was allowing me to marry his only daughter. She hugged her dad goodbye and then turned to me, and I knew this was the beginning of a new lifetime for both of us.

As we turned around to face the preacher, my mind was clear and I checked my zipper. It was never unzipped. Thanks, Gordon.

With the zipper business behind us the wedding continued without a hitch.

Pastor Kopp was wonderful and brought us together on another level that has lasted for almost fifty years. The celebration in the gymnasium was great, with a lot of people to meet and hug and all that stuff.

After a while, Phyllis and I started looking at each other with those unspoken words, "How soon can we get out of here?" We hadn't been married long and I was amazed how I understood her moving lips.

What was not known by those at the church was the party that had been secretly planned for the young people in the wedding party at the home of her best friend Joan not far away.

We finally got away and went to the party, and joined the gang that was way ahead of us in their celebrating. It didn't take us long to again start looking at each other with those unspoken words: "Let's get the heck out of here and get this honeymoon started."

We jumped in the car, waved goodbye, and were off to where our romance started: Los Angeles International Airport (LAX). This time, it was different; we were going to a hotel.

We stayed in a great room at the International Hotel right next to Los Angeles International Airport. The hotel was located between two runways and the view was spectacular with the jets taking off and landing. I tried to tell Phyllis all the things I had learned about being an air traffic controller. For some reason, she wasn't interested in what I had to say.

There are many ways I could describe our first married evening together. After thinking about it, I've decided to leave it to your imagination.

I was so glad I had a thirty day leave before going to Alaska, and couldn't wait to get started in the morning. I was up early as usual and just sat for a while watching my new bride and companion sleep. What a picture to remember.

I snuck out of the room to get some coffee and read the paper while Phyllis got her beauty sleep. When I returned she was just waking up and I couldn't stop thinking about the great adventure that was ahead of us.

As we were getting ready to go downstairs for a leisurely breakfast, Phyllis came out of the bathroom to tell me there was a telephone next to the toilet. Boy, was that exciting! We decided that after breakfast we would call several of our friends in the wedding party and let them know how special we were to have a phone in our bathroom. We hurried through breakfast, went back to our room and called several people while I sat on the toilet and Phyllis sat on the side of the tub.

At that point, we remembered that the honeymoon was just beginning and we had better hit the road. We checked out and received our bill for the one night stay. It came to $26. We loaded up the baby blue Pontiac Bonneville and were off to Santa Barbara, about 100 miles up the coast.

So many people had told me how great the Miramar Resort in Santa Barbara was and how it was right on the beach. Since we were going up the coast, I had made the reservations for two nights on the beach so we could relax and unwind after the wedding. When we checked in, I was very disappointed when I was shown a tiny bungalow way off the beach. That wasn't to be and with some negotiating, we were moved to a beachfront suite with a view of the ocean that took our breath away. We didn't go out that evening for dinner, we just called the restaurant, ordered a great meal and it was delivered by a gentleman on a bicycle who had to be in his seventies.

I stepped outside a few minutes before he arrived and I couldn't believe he was carrying our dinner on a tray on top of his head while holding the handlebar with his other hand. It was amazing and so was the meal with my new bride. Wow.

The Miramar Resort turned out to be such a great place, we decided to book the resort for one more night when we came back down the coast on our way to Disneyland. The price was tough to beat at only $24 per night.

On the third day of our honeymoon we were off to the Madonna Inn in San Louis Obispo, just off Highway 101. We had been told that it was "some place we just had to see". We already had reservations and weren't in a big hurry, so we decided to stop in Solvang, California, where we had bought our first china place setting before we were married.

It was great taking the time out to visit such a romantic Danish town and it brought back many memories of when we were dating.

On our way back to Highway 101, we decided to stop at Pea Soup Andersen's famous restaurant and have some great soup, and relax. After lunch we decided to go down to the wine cellar and take a look around. The visit turned into buying a bottle of strawberry wine that we would take with us to the Madonna Inn. It sounded like a good idea and we did it.

We then realized that we still had seventy miles to drive to get to the Madonna Inn before someone else took our reservations because we were late. I put the pedal to the metal and we cruised to the Inn with plenty of time to spare.

Our reservation was for the "Desert Sands" room with a cost of only $16 per night. We got the keys and went directly to the room to see what it looked like. When we opened the door, it was like we were walking into a desert oasis, complete with rocks for decorations, air conditioning, and it even had a bed. Our friends had told us it was a great place and it was.

We unloaded the car and got settled for our two night stay in our oasis. As we unpacked, we remembered our purchase of strawberry wine back in Solvang and decided we should open the wine and make a toast to ourselves for planning such a fantastic honeymoon.

We then discovered we didn't have a corkscrew to open the wine and it wasn't cold. It took me about two seconds to spring into action. I grabbed the ice bucket and went down to the front desk and borrowed a corkscrew. That all worked out well and I was back in our room within five minutes.

With our bucket of ice, our plastic cups and the strawberry wine, we thought we were set for the evening. It didn't take long for us to realize that mixing our strawberry wine with 7-up was not a good idea and decided to do something else.

The next day included a trip to Hearst Castle, forty-two miles up the beautiful coast on Highway 1. I hadn't planned for driving on a narrow and winding road and it took us almost two hours to reach the castle. We then discovered two problems. It was only $2 to visit the castle, which was good, but we needed reservations and we didn't have one. So, we made reservations for the next day, jumped into the car and had some second thoughts about the strawberry wine.

Our return to Hearst Castle the next day was spectacular and far beyond what we had imagined. The tour took us two and a half hours, and every moment was a new adventure we will never forget.

After another enchanted evening in our desert oasis, it was time to head south for another overnight stay at the Miramar Resort in Santa Barbara. We spent our afternoon and evening seeing the sights and having a great dinner on the wharf. We did have some wine and it wasn't strawberry.

On September 18th, we realized we had been married six days and were still speaking to each other... oh what joy!

We got an early start in the morning, coming back to the Los Angeles area on our way to the Disneyland Hotel in Anaheim where we had reservations for the 18th and 19th. We had a great room in the hotel tower and the cost was only $22 per night.

On the 19th, we spent one of those magical days doing all the things we had done years before and loving every minute of it. We spent time talking about the future and how we were going to handle being apart as I went off to Alaska to my Air Force job. At the time, I had no idea if Phyllis was going to be able to join me, and what had to be done so she could.

The 20th finally rolled around and it was time to pack up and head back to where our families lived, and try to find an apartment where we could spend our last ten days before I was off to the State of Alaska and the frozen north.

Bill's Bonneville

Bill's Departure for Alaska

Bill's Departure

Wedding Cake

Leaving Church with Top Hat

The Wedding Party

Wedding Centre Isle

Dear Miss Lloyd

Can you take a sitting
for the head at the
R— A— on Tuesday
next? If so will
you be at the schools
at a quarter before
ten.

Yours truly
D. W. Wainwright

33

..., einer Wall, ...

... bestehen ...

... emann,

Wolkramshausen

17. Merz 183..
5. Mai

schreiben: Fünfzig Thaler

...rant ... Hälfte, ...

... von Wurmbschen Güter abgeschrieben

..., ex decreto vom 25. Februar 1831 denen

... zugeschrieben.

# Chapter 4

We're Going to Alaska?
September 1964

*S*o, there I was, at the tender age of twenty-three, returning to California as an "Airman-Zero" in the Air Force to get married to the love of my life, Phyllis, going on a great honeymoon up the California coastline then returning to the Magic Kingdom at Disneyland to finish.

Silly me, thinking that could go on forever. The last two weeks of the wedding and honeymoon have been etched in my memory and I wouldn't change a thing.

I knew in the back of my mind that the thirty day leave would soon come to an end and the reality of what was ahead had to be dealt with. I remember looking in the mirror one morning and the guy looking back at me said, "Hey, you had better get off your butt and wrap up what has to be done in the next seven days or you're in big trouble."

I wasn't in a position to choose what I was going to do. The orders had been cut, my leave was almost over and I had to be in Fairbanks, Alaska, 3345 miles from my new bride by October 1st or they would come looking for me.

I had a list of things that had to do and I began to panic.

- ✔ I had to find my Air Force uniform that I had worn home.

- ✔ I had to find my duffle bag of cold weather clothes for Alaska that was sent home with me from Biloxi, Mississippi.

- ✔ I had to find all my military paperwork including orders, tickets and where to report on my arrival.

- ✔ I had to find out how to get to Eielson AFB, twenty-two miles from Fairbanks.

How was I going to do all this stuff so quickly and still have time to plan for Phyllis' arrival. I had no idea if Phyllis could even join me.

It seemed that October 1st arrived at the speed of light and we were off to Los Angeles Airport to send me to the great unknown in Alaska. To say that I was brave and up to the challenge would be a lie. To say that I was scared to death and shed more than a few tears would be the truth. How could I leave my new bride behind? I had no choice.

# Alaska

onday October 2nd, I reported for duty as an air traffic controller and was assigned to my training supervisor. I met Bobby A, my new boss, and we went to the control tower to see where I was going to work. It was seven stories high and had a great view of all the runways and surrounding landscape. I asked what we were supposed to do if we had an earthquake. He told me he would tell me some day and he never did.

Tuesday October 3rd was the first day of work and I was told to report to the tower at 8am sharp. When I arrived I met Paul Colley, who was part of our controller team and was an Airman Third Class and one rank above me, an Airman Zero (as I loved to call it).

Paul and I became great friends and he was my go-to-guy to get all the info I needed to bring Phyllis to Alaska. It wasn't an easy thing to do. For some reason, Fairbanks, Alaska, was considered to be "overseas" and I needed to get permission from my CO to bring Phyllis up.

First, I had to find Phyllis a job. Paul's wife had gone to work for Alaska National Bank and his wife, June, told me who to see at the bank. I contacted the bank and spoke with the manager about Phyllis and he said, "Bring her up. We always need experienced tellers that are good at what they do."

Next, I had to find a car with a working heater to get me back and forth to the base. I found one on base, a 1955 Chevy that didn't look so good, but it had a working heater so I bought it for $300.

Then I had to find a place we could live, and it wasn't going to be in the car I had just bought. I checked out many places and finally decided on a small one-bedroom upstairs apartment that we could call our own, and settle down to the long winter nights ahead. The cost was $200 per month. I think the whole apartment was only 400 square feet, and I had to turn sideways just to get into bed.

To this day I'm still amazed at how quickly I was able to accomplish all the things that had to be done. I returned to my commanding officer, shared my results, and he approved my request to bring Phyllis to Alaska.

The quickest that Phyllis could do all the things she needed to do; quit her job, move out of the apartment she had with her best friend, Virginia, and make airplane reservations would put her in Fairbanks on October 31st: Halloween. I wondered if the evening would be a trick or a treat. It ended up being both!

On the 31st, Phyllis' flight plan took her from Los Angeles direct to Seattle and then connected with a flight to Fairbanks. That was great with me but it wasn't great for her. As her flight departed from Seattle, two of the plane's tires blew out and they had to fly out over water and dump fuel so they could return for an emergency landing. I can't imagine what thoughts must have been running through her mind. The beginning of a new marriage far away from home where the temperatures are below zero and the sunlight disappears quickly every day.

Sitting at the airport in Fairbanks, I had no idea any of this was happening and I couldn't understand why the flight's arrival was getting later and later. I actually got permission to go up into the control tower to find out more information on her flight. All they knew was the flight was delayed because of technical difficulties. What the heck did that mean?

Phyllis finally arrived three hours late and we were both in tears. I got the full story about dumping the fuel and landing with two blown tires. They could have come to Fairbanks, but there were no tires in Fairbanks.

Finally, after too many days and too many hours, we were together again and freezing our behinds off. I had no problem with the temperature when Phyllis arrived. I had been there almost four weeks and with the clothes supplied by the Air Force I was fine. On the other hand, Phyllis was not and I had the feeling that the California girl wanted to go home.

Phyllis had gotten on the plane in Los Angeles where it was eighty degrees, changed planes in Seattle where it was sixty degrees and got off this flight where it was ZERO.

The important thing was that Phyllis was in my arms, trying to warm up and she was taking her first ride in our 1955 Chevy with the heater going full blast.

Halloween night in Fairbanks, Alaska, is not to exciting because of the COLD, COLD, COLD. The young children that did go out all wore knitted face masks and you didn't know who they were anyway. I think we may have had 3 children at our door. I was okay with that because Phyllis and I were back together again.

The Monday following Halloween was an important day. Phyllis was going to the bank to get the job the manager had promised me she would have.

Phyllis got out of the car shortly after 10am and went into the bank to meet with the manager. She wasn't in there very long and came out with tears running down her face. I will never forget it. Even though they had promised her a job, they had put a freeze on all hiring until spring rolled around and there was nothing that could be done.

I said a few choice words about the bank and their manager. The bank's decision created a major problem for us since Phyllis had to have a job to be able to come to Alaska. Now what would we do? Phyllis didn't have a job, we had bought a car, rented an apartment and everything was great until the bank backed out of their promise.

The one thing I knew for sure was that Phyllis was there to stay and I would do everything in my power to make it happen.

Looking for a job when the sun is out and its eighty degrees is one thing. Looking for a job when the sun is only up for two hours each day and the old thermometer says it's below zero degrees is no easy task when your hands and feet are freezing. Having a desire to do the right thing and having a plan to accomplish your goals don't always match up. We took on this new battle, looking for any job that needed to be filled.

Phyllis first contacted the Alaska Unemployment Department looking for job listings and getting information on what may be needed to receive unemployment benefits because of her move from California to be with her husband. Fortunately for Phyllis, the gentleman that helped her took a real interest in our problem, did some checking into military dependents who moved into the state, found some way that Phyllis qualified for Alaska's unemployment program and signed her up. She was also told that if she found a job, she could work plus receive the benefits. I had no idea this was possible and I didn't ask questions.

Phyllis found several jobs, working for the University of Alaska doing computer data entry and at the Travelers Inn running the front desk.

So what the heck was I doing to support the family? Next to Fairbanks was Fort Wainwright. The Army had a commissary store where army families bought groceries for their homes. If you could stand the cold, you could help people out to their cars in the cold and snow for tips. They were always looking for people and I was just the right guy to get the job done. The Army got paid twice a month, and on payday I could make $30 to $40 dollars in tips in about three hours which really helped us out.

To say the least, our first winter in the great State of Alaska was tough with jobs not coming easily and not long in duration. We learned what it meant to work together, count our blessings and our pennies, and do whatever it took so we could be together.

It didn't take us long to learn what the people of Alaska were all about, doing for others and helping friends to survive in the bitterly cold winters. We were told that spring was not far away and we would quickly forget about the cold at forty degrees below zero.

As we began to adjust to our new surroundings, we quickly learned what had to be done to take care of our car and keep it running in the below zero temperatures. First, every car needed to have a Head Bolt Heater installed in the engine that kept the engine oil from freezing. At our apartment we had our own plug-in receptacle to plug our car in when we got home. The next thing we learned was the importance of finding electrical outlets around town that you could plug your car into.

One evening we went to the one movie theatre in Fairbanks to see a James Bond flick and there were six people in our car. We parked not far from the theatre and took turns standing in line to buy tickets because there was nowhere to plug our car in. That made for a fun evening with all of us jumping in and out of the car.

Next, we learned the importance of having the right clothes that gave us protection from the cold. It was easy for me, since the Air Force provided me with what they called "fat boy pants" and a parka. It wasn't easy to get into but it kept me warm when I had to go outside.

On the other hand, we had to get the right clothes for Phyllis and ended up getting her lots of ladies long underwear and a warm parka, which she still has to this day, and it's too warm to wear until it gets down below zero which it rarely does.

As the days got shorter and we adjusted to our home away from home for the next twenty months, the holidays were upon us with Thanksgiving just around the corner and Christmas not far away.

The menu we chose for dinner went right along with our apartment. It was Cornish Game hens that were small, just like the apartment. There was no way we could afford a turkey and we didn't have an oven that the turkey could fit in. We truly enjoyed the afternoon and evening and we gave thanks for being inside where it was warm and cozy.

With Thanksgiving behind us and Christmas on the way we decided that we needed lights and ornaments to decorate our first Christmas tree. We asked our friends where we could get our Christmas tree, thinking someone might say, "Go out in the woods and cut it down." That didn't happen because Christmas trees didn't grow in Alaska! What a shock that was. We then learned that all the Christmas trees were imported from Montana and we could find them at the market.

As I mentioned before, our apartment was so tiny that we weren't sure if we could find a tree that would fit. Because of the cold outside, we chose one quickly and brought it home. It seemed to take up half the room when we got the lights and decorations on it.

We soon learned another lesson about Christmas trees in Alaska. When you bring a tree indoors that has been outside in below zero temperatures, it doesn't take long for it to die. I think it may have taken two to three days at the most.

Since it was Christmas, we decided to invite Ralph Luke, a fellow controller, over for dinner. Ralph and I were in the same class at the air traffic controller school. Since Ralph was from Montana and I was from California, we ended up being the only people who lived on the West Coast, so they shipped us to Alaska. Thanks a lot!

One great thing we learned about our new home in Alaska was that we were just twenty miles from North Pole, Alaska. This little town had been turned into the semi-official place where Santa lives and makes all his gifts. The North Pole had a post office where we could mail all our Christmas cards from. For an extra $5, you could send a letter from Santa to your relatives saying whatever you wanted Santa to say. Each letter or package had a big stamp on that said: From North Pole, Alaska.

The most important thing we learned about Christmas Day was that it was the shortest day during the winter and each new day we gained more sunlight on its way to summer when the sun never went down.

That really helped us make it through our first cold winter.

*I hope you brought your parka
and snow shoes.
It's minus 22 degrees.
Baby it's cold outside!*

1st Home - Fairbanks, Alaska

Anselment Family Dinner

Bobby Anselment Family

Cabbage Head Bill

Gold Rush Days Costumes

Phyllis in her Can Can Outfit

Phyllis on Parade Float

Phyllis and The Bee Hive

Phyllis with a Big Bear!

Phyllis-Look at that Hair!

*Phyllis with Alaskan Cabbage*

Dear Miss Lloyd

Can you take a sitting for the head at the R----- on Tuesday next? If so will you be at the schools at a quarter to ten.

Yours truly

J. W. Waterhouse

My dear Dixie

"The Children's Treasury" books large ... tons of England ... I intend reading ... children ... I do not like little folks this evening because I want to ... our old copy was cleaning badly ... the Round game ... understand it now ... kind love

Wolkramshausen
17. März
5. Mai
ex decreto vom 25. Februar

# CHAPTER 5

Alaska's...
"Serious ATC Business"

s most of you have noticed, I haven't said much about the reason I was sent to Alaska. When they asked me at Tech School where I wanted to be sent for my 1st assignment, I told them that Germany or France might be nice. The decision makers must have had a great laugh at my request and decided to give me a "Really Cool" opportunity in Alaska of all places.

I went into the Air Force February 1964. At the time, it was mandatory for all men when 18 to register for the draft. I enlisted in the Air Force at the age of 23 for four years, went through basic training at Lackland AFB in San Antonio, Texas.

I attended Air Traffic Control School in Biloxi, Mississippi for six months, graduated and returned to California to get married on September 12, 1964.

## "Cleared for Take-Off"

y first military base assignment was Eielson Air Force Base that was located 22 miles outside the city of Fairbanks, Alaska. Getting to and from work was not an easy task on a two lane highway in those winter nights. The Air force had supplied me with a Great hooded parka and Fat Boy Pants for my comfort.

When you learned how to wear the parka, you could actually zip it so far that your face didn't show.

Since Phyllis's arrival, we had bought a newer car and our little red & white Ford Falcon station wagon was well equipped for any emergency that I may run into while on the road. The front of the radiator was covered with aluminum foil so the engine would heat up the inside of the car. Just behind the front seat, I installed a clear plastic barrier to keep the front of the car warm. Next, I carried 5 gallons of gas and some road flares just in case I got stuck on the road and had to stay warm or someone needed my help.

As Air Traffic Controllers, we worked five day a week on three rotating shifts which changed every week; days, swing shift and mid-shifts.

Our Control Tower was seven stories high which gave us a great view of the airport and runway. The runway was 15,600ft long (that's almost 3 miles) and 300 feet wide.

Our primary Military Mission was to launch and recover the KC-135 Ariel Refueling tankers that were supporting the B-52 Bombers that were in the air 24 hours a day to keep our country safe.

I assigned to work with SGT. Bobby A. He would be responsible for all my training until I became a fully-qualified controller. It was incredible what I had to learn to be part of the team and the amount of reading that was required to be a fully qualified Air Traffic Controller.

As an Airman-Zero, I quickly found out that what I had learned at the Air Traffic Control school in Mississippi only scratched the surface of what I needed to do to be "Qualified" to step into the number 1 position in the tower.

One floor below us were all the tape recorders that ran 24 hours a day to record every word that was spoken by us and the pilots we were in contact with.

The most important part of my learning were the exact words that had to come out of my mouth to give instructions to the pilots when they were flying in my controlled Air Space at the Airport.

There was no room for excuses and It had to be done right the first time and every time.

Way back in 1964, working in the control tower was nothing that you would see today. There were no radar screens in the tower to locate the incoming aircraft and there were no computer screens showing their distance from the airport.

All of this had to be done by the Senior Controller, with his microphone in hand, using his eyes and experience to make it all happen safely. There was no room for making mistakes when you were dealing with million dollar aircraft landing at your airport at 100+ miles per hour. This was the number one priority of the Senior Controller on the shift.

In addition, the senior controller was assisted by two assistant-controllers keeping track of the arriving planes and directing them to their final parking spot. All vehicles, including the Fire Department were in contact with the tower at all times.

Refueling our B-52 Bombers was our number one priority. We had twelve KC-135 aerial tankers on base to do the job and it was critical to get them airborne on time. Many times on their regular departure schedules, we had moose jump over the fences surrounding the airport and end up causing delays in their departures.

When this happened, we had to close the runway to all departures until the airport security team rushed to where the moose were and used their flair guns to encourage the moose to depart. For some reason, which was not a pretty sight, they got the message and were on their way quickly. We cleared the re-fueling tankers into position for take-off and they were on their way to meet up with the B-52's.

At the south end of the airport, was the home of the Alaska Air Defense Command. It was comprised of 4 F-102 fighter jets in their own hangers always ready to make an immediate departure to protect our B-52 Bombers in flight and any potential attack on the airport.

Located in Anchorage Alaska, was Elmendorf AFB which had the same type of fighter jets and would practice their scramble departures two to three times per week. The procedure was always the same. One of the training jets would depart 20-30 minutes to parts unknown and then two fighter jets would "Scramble" to practice their procedures to locate their target and lock on for firing.

When the aircraft had finished their training, they always paid us a visit at Eielson to practice their "Simulated Flame-Out" approach starting at 10,000 feet in a spiral which ended up coming over the active end of the runway. Each pilot would report "High-Key" at 10,000 feet, cleared to "Low-Key" at 5,000 feet, and then be cleared to land as they were on the final approach to the runway.

One day, I had 3 aircraft in the approach pattern at the same time and it was both exciting and intense at the same time. The entire procedure for each aircraft took less than 3 minutes to accomplish.

As you may imagine, as we learned to work with each other under the pressure of the Control Tower, we came to trust each other and became a close knit team.

When I became a fully-rated Tower Controller, my teacher, Bobby A. was always watching me closely and listening to the instructions I gave the pilots. When I did say something wrong, Bobby would wack me on the side of my head... and tell me he was using his "Rolled-up Newspaper" method of teaching. It didn't take long for me to get all the words perfect.

When we had been together for about 6 months, Bobby advised me that when just the two of us were working the midnight shift, it was his plan to lie on the floor with his blanket and pillow and go to sleep... And when I became "Fully Rated", we would then take turns sleeping. That sounded like a great idea for me and I studied even harder to get rated.

On one midnight shift, Bobby was asleep on the floor while I was reading the controller manuals so I could take advantage of his offer.

The Control Tower had a Bright Red telephone right in the middle of our control center. The reason for the phone was simple. If it ever rang I was to pick up the phone immediately because the Air Defense Command was "Scrambling" an F-102 Fighter Jet to intercept a potential foreign aircraft that was within our protected airspace.

As the phone was still ringing, I was yelling at Bobby... to wake him up... which didn't happen... which meant that I was in complete control of this fighters launch to parts unknown. I had to stop yelling at Bobby because the pilot was beginning his taxi out to the runway for his departure. He came on his radio and said, "Tower... Tower, this is X-ray PaPa 01". He was stuttering because he had never been on a "Real-Scramble" in his life.

When the call sign was "XRay-Papa", it meant that the aircraft was armed with "Nuclear Missiles".

What he didn't know was that he was talking to a controller who had never done this before either. I picked up my microphone and said, "Roger-Roger" X-ray Papa 01... as I was stuttering and scared to death.

I must have tried to wake Bobby up several more times and I was still on my own. I gave him his departure instructions and I was ready to clear him for take-off when the "Scramble" phone went off again cancelling his departure and sending him back to the hanger.

As soon as I had cancelled his departure, both of our voices stopped stuttering and we got back to normal.

Finally, I went over and woke Bobby up from a deep sleep and told him what had just happened and asked if I had done things right? He actually said it was "Great".

Bobby was now awake, got himself a cup of coffee and lit up his cigarette and we discussed other departure stories he had been involved in. It didn't take him long to finish the coffee and cigarette and stretch out on the floor again and go sound asleep again.

I had my coffee and cigarette and was getting back into my assigned reading when the "Red Phone" went off again and another fighter cam rolling out of the hanger. It had to be a new pilot he was stuttering just like the last pilot and said "Tower, Tower, X-ray Papa 02, ready for departure". Since I had all the experience of doing this before, I was cool and collected as I gave him his departure instructions. He rolled onto the runway, went to "After Burner" and disappeared into the night sky.

To this day, I can still remember the fear and excitement of those two experiences in the same evening. When I had calmed down, I wrote my Mom & Dad a letter and told them that If a war comes soon, please don't tell them that I cleared the fighter jet with Nuclear Missiles to take off.

On the brighter side, one of the perks we had while we were at work, was the "In-Flight" kitchen at the base of the tower where there was a full-time staff making meals for the pilots and crews on their long refueling missions.

As we got ready to take the elevator, we would always say hi to the cooks and let them know they could come up to the tower anytime they wanted... which they liked. When they did call, we always asked if they had any food that didn't go with the flight crews? It was always amazing how many goodies they always brought up and I think we all gained 5-10 pounds every winter.

Working the day shifts on the weekend with Bobby was always fun and he wanted me to experience things outside of the control tower. I got invited to go on a training flight on one of the KC-135's as the pilots practiced their take-offs and landings. I was in the cockpit seated on a jump seat between the pilot and co-pilot. It was really a Big Deal for me and I realized what had to be done to get their aircraft on the runway.

# MY TRIBUTE TO THE
# "ROLLED-UP" NEWSPAPER GUY!

Working with Bobby, my Boss and my mentor, was all serious business when we worked together in the Control Tower.

For some unknown reason, we connected from the first time we met and he became my "Away from home Dad". Of Course he was much older than I was and at times he said that he "Knew Everything" and he could prove it.

Who was I, at the age of 23 to question my 45 year old boss that had lived in Alaska for years and was never going to leave.

We spent many hours in the Control Tower and our friendship grew to a point that we were invited to join his family at home and go on outings during the summer when it was light 24 hours a day.

I remember driving back to Fairbanks one day from the base in our 1961 Ford Falcon Station Wagon when a red light came on the dash board. I remember banging on the dashboard with my fist to get the red light to go out which it didn't. I pulled over, turned off the car and then tried again... same result.

I was not far from the base in "North Pole", Alaska "Believe it or not". I called Bobby at his home and told him what had happened. He told me not to do anything and he would be right there and take a look. Twenty minutes later, there he was with his tool box, asked me what happened and checked out the problem. He told me the oil pump had gone out and it needed to be fixed.

Being young and broke most of the time, with Phyllis and I struggling to make ends meet, Bobby used one of his familiar sayings, "No Problem" and we could fix it right here at the base at the auto repair shop that I didn't know was there. We then towed the car to the shop, got the needed parts and we worked together to fix the car that afternoon.

On one of our camping trips with his family, Bobby had brought several of his guns so we could do some target practice which was "All New to me" since I never owned a gun in my life. Bobby had a 44 Magnum revolver and asked if I wanted to "Shoot a Tree"?

Before I knew it, the gun was loaded and in my hands. Bobby said it had a "Real Kick" when it was fired and told me which tree to shoot at. I did and the kick almost dislocated my shoulder... when they asked me again and I said NO !!!!

Then Bobby asked me if I had ever been hunting, which I hadn't. He asked me if I wanted to go Caribou hunting in the fall and it would be fun. All I needed was a rifle and I could buy it really cheap at the PX at the Army Fort. To this day, I don't know why I bought a rifle... except to experience something new with a great friend.

It didn't take long for the leaves to change color and the weather to get colder for Bobby to let me know that the time had come to "Go Hunting". I had no ideas what was going to happen.

We headed north on the Steese Highway out of town as it got darker. The further we drove the more it snowed and I was wondering what I had gotten myself into. We came to a curve in the road where there was a level place where we could park the car, have something to eat and get some sleep.

Have you ever tried to sleep in the back of a Chevrolet Station Wagon with no padding to lay on and no place to go to the bathroom? I remember standing on the doorway and trying to do my thing.

I must have survived and morning seemed to come quickly. It had snowed all night and as we looked around, we had parked at the base of a Caribou Trail in the dark. As it got lighter, it didn't take long for several Caribou to come over the rise and walk in our direction. I had taken lessons from Bobby on how to load the rifle and was read to shoot when they got closer.

On my first shot, I missed. On my second shot I didn't. Then I realized what I had done and I "Cried".

Thinking back, I have no idea if Bobby was letting me experience the hunting and the killing of an animal on my own. He never said a word and he never asked what my thoughts were.

The rest of the day seemed to go quickly. I got another Caribou and Bobby his own. Once again I had no idea what was coming next... Preparing to take our 3 caribou back to Fairbanks, each animal had to be cleaned before we took our trophy's home.

It seemed like the trip back with the Caribou hanging out of the car took a long time for me to think about what just happen. It was an experience that I never plan to do again...

Once we arrived home, our landlord Tony volunteered to help me cut up and wrap the caribou meat. Not a pleasant site to deal with. With it beginning to get very cold, Tony gave me an old trunk that we could store the meat in outside the back door of our apartment. Everyone was happy to take their share of the meat and Toni's wife Irene cooked us several dinners during the winter. Even with all spices that were used in the cooking, it was not our favorite meal when we went over for dinner.

The Air Traffic Controller training I received from my teacher while I was stationed in Alaska has served me well and I have to thank my friend and mentor Bobby and his "Rolled-Up" newspaper teaching method which I think about often.

To many, Alaska may seem like a cold and difficult state to live in with all its sub-zero temperature days that we hear so much about. What we don't hear enough about are the kind and loving people that live there year round and can't do enough to make you and your families "Welcome" if given a chance.

On a scale of 1-10, our experience was a True 15 and I will never forget it.

*My air traffic controller job…*
*no room for mistakes!*
*Lives were at stake.*
*On the Nuclear Edge.*

# CHAPTER 6

"THE LOWER 48"

*I*n April of 1966, we were informed that my next Air Force assignment was somewhere in Northern California and the name of the town was Yreka. We were so excited; it was hard to find a map to see where it was. When we finally got a map, we could find Eureka, California on the coast but no Yreka. Did they just spell the name wrong? We had no clue.

We were excited to return to the "Lower-48", after being in Alaska for 20 months. When we did find Yreka on the map, we found out the population was only 5,000 people. At first we were disappointed until we realized that we were actually back in the "Lower 48 States" and closer to our friends and families in sunny Southern California.

With us still driving our 1961 Ford Falcon Station wagon in Fairbanks, Alaska, we made the decision to sell the car and order a new one from a Military Car Dealer that was doing business from Portland Oregon. We got the brochures within a week, read them from cover to cover and decided to buy a 1966 Buick Station Wagon. We only made two mistakes when we placed the order. We forgot where we where we were going and ordered a Dark Blue car with heavy duty 8-ply tires that would have been great if we were staying in Fairbanks... and we weren't...

We still have many great memories that will last forever including all the people we shared the cold-cold winters and the spectacular summers in the 20 months we were there. It seemed like they could never do enough for you and would ask nothing in return. Wow, how things have changed in our lives since way back in 1966.

We did share more than a few tears as our plane taxied out for departure. We had a direct flight to Seattle which took about four hours. We were both amazed how big the city was and we were anxious to get our feet on the ground.

I'm not sure how we made it through Sea Tac Airport. It must have been all my Air Traffic Controller training. We rode the shuttle bus from the airport to the Roosevelt Hotel where we had made reservations. We wanted to stay downtown, have a great dinner and just look at all the tall buildings.

The next morning, we had an early flight to Portland, Oregon to pick up the car and the person who sold us the car was picking us up at the airport and taking us directly to the dealer where the car was. It was great!!!

Since it was the Memorial Day weekend, the car dealer was closed and the sales person had been given the key to the repair shop where the car was ready to go and so were we. It was our 1966, Dark Blue, Buick Station Wagon with a luggage rack on top... It was so cool and it was full of gas...

Since it was the holiday weekend, it was a little dark in the shop which made no difference as we did our "walk-around" to check out the car. That took a total of 5 minutes... and everything looked "Ok". It even had Oregon license plates on the car...

We signed the final papers, and were given the directions to the freeway which was just down the road, I started the engine, turned on the radio and we were off to a brand new adventure in our brand new car... What could be better.

At the southern end of the state was our destination, Yreka, California and it was only 322 miles away and we could be there in only 4 hours and 39 minutes. There was no question in our minds what we were going to do, drive there in 4 hours and 30 minutes... "And Be Home"...

The ride was great, the music coming from the radio was superb and we were "Almost Staying" under the speed limit.

When we were 220 miles south of Portland, we decided to get a burger and a coke at the next town which was only 30 miles down the road. We pulled into a McDonalds, leaped out of the car and hustled into the restroom. We got our food, walked out the door, and took a stroll around our Brand New Car. When we got to the hood of the car, something just wasn't right, the Dark Blue color on the engine hood... just wasn't "Dark Blue" like the rest of the car. I took a few bites of my Big Mac and then I realized that way back in Portland, our car had been in the repair shop and no lights had been on... The salesman knew that the paint job wasn't right and he had moved the car indoors where we couldn't see the bad paint job.

Here we were, almost to Yreka on a holiday weekend and our New Car Wasn't Perfect!!!! After a few tears and a few more bites of the cheese burgers, we decided there was no way we were going back... and decided to press-on to Yreka... they had to have a Buick Car Dealer there, didn't they????

The last 102 miles seemed to take forever with both of us constantly looking out the front window hoping that something magic would happen to the hood of our car.

We finally pulled into the City of Yreka. No, there wasn't a Buick Car Dealer... the town only had one stop light .and not much of anything else. After asking around we did find the "One & Only" motel and got a room for the night.

We just couldn't handle any more... for one day!!!!!!

As we drifted off to sleep, we just had to wonder what the next day would bring.

When you're in the military and moving to a new assignment or base, you are put in touch with someone to help you find housing to make a smooth transition. It was my job to get in touch with them, introduce myself, let them know when we would be arriving and get an address to ship our household goods to that they would put in storage till we arrived.

We followed all the rules because we had no idea where we were going. We shipped all our household goods thirty days before departure to Yreka and hoped that they would make it before we did.

In addition, we gave them an idea what we were looking for in an apartment and the price range that we could afford at my current pay rate. This I did and we felt comfortable when we shipped our limited amount of household goods off 30 days in advance of our departure from Fairbanks.

Three weeks after our goods were shipped, we received word that the correct number of boxes had arrived and were put in storage at their home.

Since our arrival was on a Friday afternoon and we had found a comfortable motel to stay in, we decided to spend the weekend exploring Yreka and the surrounding area prior to meeting with our contact the following Monday...

We checked out the entire town looking for that Buick Car Dealer which wasn't there, we went through the one and only traffic light many times; we found a Denny's and the Elks Club where we could eat and found a few apartments that might meet our needs. Since I couldn't wait, we even found the airport where I would be working controlling those important United States Air Force Jets.

When Monday morning rolled around, we were anxious to get started finding a place to live and got together with our Air Force contact to take a look at what he had found.

The apartment was downtown, up a flight of stairs, in a building that looked like it was built in the 1920's. It shouldn't have surprised us; all the buildings looked the same. All of our boxes were there and we were happy that they made it.

As we started to look around the apartment, we checked out the kitchen and found a few things that just wouldn't work for us. The kitchen sink was so low that we would have had to sit in a chair to wash the dishes. Not Good! Then there was the problem with the kitchen light that was just a light bulb on the end of a wire. Not Good Either...

Yes, we were almost home to Southern California, sitting in a one bedroom apartment that was built in the 1920's and we had already paid the 1st month's rent! It truly wasn't what we had planned for coming back to the "Lower-48"...

It only took us 30 seconds to decide that this historic apartment wasn't for us and we started to do some serious looking for a great apartment.

The next morning, we awoke with a mission to accomplish, find a place to live in our price range that had electricity, running water and was built in this century. It didn't take long... In fact it was just 124 brisk steps up the hill and across the street and there it was; a New, two bedroom apartment, up a flight of new stairs and made just for us. Finally, we had a place we could call home.

With the help of some new found friends in the Air Force, it didn't take us long to move our household goods up the street into our new apartment.

So here we were, in Yreka, California, in a new apartment with no bed, no couch, no kitchen table, no chairs, no lamps and ten large boxes of household goods that needed to go somewhere when we got our new furniture which we hadn't started looking for.

Four things that we did have were; a New Buick Station Wagon, a comfortable motel room, we had each other and 20 days left of our vacation leave before I had to report for duty at the Air Force.

We took a break and went to dinner to discuss what our next move would be. We laughed and cried about what we had been through in the past 10 days and decided to pack up our bags and head for Southern California. We checked the maps and mileage and it was only 652 miles away and it wouldn't take us long to get there. We decided to go early in the morning and packed our bags for a quick getaway.

It took us a total of two days to get back to Los Angeles and I was amazed how things had changed and it actually frightened me to be on the freeway with all those crazy people. Where did they all come from? Had we been gone that long?

On a wing and a prayer, we actually made it to my parent's house in Huntington Park and even drove past Sears & Roebucks where my parents had worked for many years and my old High School where I went to school way back in 1958.

Once we were in town, things got hectic. We did all those crying and hugging things at my parent's house and then it was time to get to Phyllis's house to do all the hugging again.

Phyllis's parent's lived in South Gate where Phyllis was born and not far from my parents. Don and Sadie had lived in the same house for many years which was built in the early 1900's complete with gas lighting in the walls. It made me think about our 1st place in Yreka which was built about the same time. I wonder if it was the same contractor.

Don and Sadie's house was where all our wedding gifts had been stored for the past 20 months while we were in Alaska and we couldn't wait to "See Again" all the great stuff we received.

We did have our "Big Blue Buick" Station Wagon to take some of them back to our new home in Yreka. In our excitement, we temporarily forgot that we didn't have enough room to put all the treasurers when we got back to Yreka. We made an executive decision to "Take them Anyway" and find room when we got home.

The gifts that had been stored were everywhere; in cupboards, under beds, in closets with lots of shelves, in the pantry with the food and it went on & on. Then I remembered that we had over 400 people at the wedding and it all made sense.

If my memory is still functioning, I think we got "16 Sets of Glasses" with 6 or 8 glasses in each set. It was total confusion just looking at all the great gifts and trying to decide what to take and what we could actually get into our shrinking "Big Blue Buick" Station Wagon without dragging the glasses behind the car!!!!!!

I have to admit being back in Southern California was turning out great reliving our wedding and all the great gifts we received. Seeing our aging parents was a little difficult but we got use to it and loved them even more.

We did take a few days to see our old high school friends when we could find them which wasn't easy. We decided to try again when we came back for a second load of "Stuff".

When we left Yreka, we had 20 days of leave left before I had to report for duty. With our 2 days going down, 2 days visiting relatives & friends and 2 more days to get back to Yreka, we only had 14 days left before I had to go to work.

It was time to load up our "Small Blue Buick Station Wagon" and head home to take care of a few things like buying all the furniture for our apartment including a bed. For some reason, we both agreed about getting a bed.

By the time we loaded up our Wagon, it was wall to wall stuff and almost impossible to see out the windows. We didn't care, we were going Home. The trip back took 2 long days. Seeing the off-ramp sign to Yreka brought a few tears of joy to finally be home.

Home sweet home looked great and we didn't care if we slept on the floor, we had each other.


As Usual, I woke up early with the thought of fresh coffee brewing in the kitchen. No such luck, we forgot to buy groceries. We decided to make a list of all that had to be done and in what order we had to do it. Saying that was easier said than done! What should go first the horse or the cart?

We were stepping into a world that we had been shielded from for the past 20 month when we were stationed in Alaska. Our apartment was furnished; we both had jobs with me in the Air force and Phyllis working at the bank. We had many friends that we knew well and were there to help us if needed.

A new reality was rushing in that we knew nothing about. We were really on our own and had to make many decisions quickly and correctly if we were to survive in this new adventure.

The list of "To Do" things included the following.

- ✔ Go to the Bank of America and see what had to be done to get a loan to buy furniture for our apartment. I didn't think I had any financial history that I could use. And I hoped that being in the Air Force would help

- ✔ Go furniture shopping to determine what we really needed for the apartment, what the cost was and what could wait?

The first list was short with each item critical.

We did agree that the only way we were going to get a loan was if we both had a job which meant Phyllis had to find one, hopefully in the Banking Business and Bill had to get a 2nd job to help pay off the loans.

We did agree that we had just been through a "Tough Time in Alaska" and we could do it again here in Yreka if we were given a chance.

One of the stores we looked at was Sears & Roebucks that had a catalogue order store in town but we had to wait for weeks before it would arrive. We continued our search and found a great furniture store that had everything we needed to get started and it could be delivered the same day.

Things were beginning to come together if all the pieces fell into place.

- ✔ The Bank of America approved our loan.
- ✔ The Furniture store still had the items we picked out.

It was time to go back to our empty apartment, say several prayers and take a break until Monday and see what happened. It was going to be a long weekend.

With all our running around to the bank and the furniture store we had used up another three days and only had 10 days left before I had to report to work at Siskiyou County Airport and check in with the Commanding Officer. It was time to get my military uniform ready to go to work.

It didn't take long for Monday to roll around as we sat on the floor and had breakfast. About 10:30am the phone rang and almost scared us to death. In my best adult voice I said "Good Morning", this is Bill Perry. It was the Bank of America calling to let us know that our loan had been "Approved" and the money was being deposited into our checking account that day.

What a joy it was to laugh and cry all at the same time when we knew we had the "Bucks" to go shopping "For Real". It didn't take us long to get to the store, find our sales person and give him our good news. We set up delivery for later in the day as they had promised they could do.

Finally, we realized that in the short span of five days we had accomplished our two major goals, getting the bank loan and ordering the furniture.

All we had to do now was go Home and clean the apartment for our delivery. We couldn't bring new furniture into a dirty apartment.

Things were beginning to move quickly now with the new furniture in our apartment. The arranging and rearranging went on until we both decided it was perfect "For Now".

With only a few days left until I started my new job, I decided to go out to the airport and meet the guys who ran the FAA flight service station.

The airport was controlled by the FAA and flights had to check in for landing instructions and then were turned over to the tower for their approach.

There were four different guys that worked for the FAA and they had been there for many years. All of them had worked at major airports in California and had wanted to move to a smaller airport which Siskiyou County seemed to be.

I was called the "New Guy" and we seemed to be on the same page with some of our stories. I'm glad that I made the effort to meet them and checking in Monday would be much easier.

Before we knew it, Friday had arrived and we decided to go out to dinner to celebrate what we had accomplished in record time. We were getting comfortable living in Yreka and looked forward to Monday's arrival.

I had called ahead to confirm my appointment time with the Commanding Officer. Vacation was over and it was time to get back to controlling all those Air Force Jets.

I had to be there at 8am sharp with all my transfer papers to be processed and hopefully be put into the control tower that I had seen across the runway. I arrived on time and was introduced to the CO.

We discussed my previous assignment in Alaska and our mission at Eielson AFB.

**Then, something happened that I didn't expect and didn't believe the question I was being asked.**

The CO wanted to know if I ever played "Fast Pitch" Softball in my life. When I said yes, he asked what position I had played. When I said that I pitched, I could see that he was smiling from "Ear to Ear".

Of course I asked why and was told that Hamilton AFB, just outside of San Francisco was getting ready to have their Championship Softball Tournament in two days and our pitcher had just retired from the Air Force and they wouldn't let him come back to pitch... and they needed me to pitch in the tournament.

After I said, "He had to be kidding several times", he assured me that he wasn't and I had better find some baseball shoes and a glove because a C-47 would be here at 07:00am to pick me up and fly me to Hamilton for the softball game.

I could hardly walk out of the office without guys I didn't know giving me Hi fives and telling me to go "Kick Butt".

I had no idea what I was going to tell Phyllis when I got home with a Big Smile on my face. I told her the story, which she didn't believe. Then I told her that I had been ordered by the CO to be at the airport at 7am for my flight to Hamilton AFB.

It didn't take long for 5am to arrive and the beginning of another adventure. I showered, shaved and out on my clean uniform. I kissed Phyllis goodbye and I was off to Siskiyou County Airport to meet my C-47 airplane ride to Hamilton Air Force near San Francisco.

I parked at the FAA flight service station and there it was the C-47 Cargo Plane waiting for my arrival.

I met the Captain and crew, climbed on board, learned the rules of flying in this aircraft and was strapped in for our departure. We taxied onto the runway, were given clearance for take-off, went to full power and rolled down the runway heading south and lifted off for our two hour flight to San Francisco.

The aircraft was a C-47 Cargo plane, totally empty inside except for me strapped in my seat. Even with my earplugs in place, it wasn't a quiet ride in the back with the engines straining to get to cruising altitude.

The view of Mount Shasta was spectacular, as we flew east of the mountain with its two peaks that use to be volcanic many years ago. At this time of the year, both peaks still had snow on them. The history that surrounded the mountain said many years ago, when the snow had disappeared from both peaks, there was volcanic eruption on one peak which spewed volcanic rocks over the entire Siskiyou Valley. The landscape of the valley is still covered with thousands of rocks.

If you ask a local resident about the history of the mountain, they will tell you that many long time residents go outside each morning and check the mountain to make sure the snow cap is still in place.

Just south of Mount Shasta was Lake Shasta with all the recreational adventures you would ever want including house boat rentals, jet skiing and of course some great fishing.

Before I knew it, we were approaching Hamilton Air Force Base and preparing for landing. With San Francisco in the distance and the Golden Gate Bridge, it was a sight that I will never forget.

Our landing was perfect and I was met by another member of our Air Traffic Control team that were stationed at Hamilton AFB.

We had a great lunch at the mess hall and talked about where I had been stationed and then we went to visit the Control Tower. The tower was about the same size as we had in Alaska and looked like home. Their runway was much shorter than in Alaska.

After visiting the Control Tower, I was taken to BOQ which stood for the Bachelor Officer Quarters which was big surprise for me since my rank was an Airman 1st Class.

How I got in there, I have no idea. I had my own room with a shower and it was great.

I guess they thought I was some great softball pitcher and wanted me to have the best... and I enjoyed it.

## "Game on... Where's the Pitcher"?

*Before we go any further, it should be noted that when I experienced this wonderful part of my life, I was 25 years old. As I write this story today from my memory, I'm 73 years old and I shouldn't be held responsible for everything being totally accurate. Thank You.*

Shortly after I arrived at Hamilton Air Force Base, we had a team meeting and I met all the guys on the team. They seemed to come from all over the place including other Air Force Bases in the San Francisco area.

We were all there because this was a "Serious" game that we were about to play and there was no way that the Air Traffic Controllers were going to lose. We all agreed and were slapping hands as we gave each other high 5's.

The Tournament turned into a 2 day affair and I was pitching the first game. I did have some time to practice the day I arrived and I was really beginning to believe that I had the talent to win the game. I borrowed a glove and some spikes and I was ready to give it my ALL!

When we arrived at the game to warm up, I watched the other team warming up and I realized that their team was made up of mostly older guys. I had to wonder how they got to the Base Championship with just old guys?

When I began warming up, I don't remember how it happened but everything I was doing was the same way that I had done it before... I asked myself how I was able to pitch since the last time I pitched. I was five years ago didn't care and just kept doing it.

If my memory serves me right, and it may not, it was a very tight game and had turned into a mini-pitching duel... Me against Him...

For some reason, the older guys on the other team didn't get their bats around quick enough and most of them struck out. Of course, this really got me "Pumped-Up" and so did the rest of the team.

In the end, we won the game 2 to 0 and I had pitched a 2 hitter... which was amazing to me. We ended up at the NCO club for a few beers to celebrate our "Glorious Victory".

By the time I got to the BOQ, I could feel my right arm beginning to change into a non-functional part of my body. What was I to do, tomorrow was another game. I spent the next hour in the shower trying to nurse my arm back to good health...

When I woke up the next morning, it was obvious to me that my pitching days had come to an END. I realized there had been no miraculous recovery during the night and there was no way I could attempt to play.

When I met with the team for breakfast and they looked at my right arm hanging down below my waist... they pretty much knew that the "Pitcher from Siskiyou" was not getting on the mound to pitch.

Yesterday, we had played the "Old Guy's, who were the best team on the base and we beat them. What happened today just didn't matter and nobody cared because of yesterday's victory!

I didn't make it to the game that day because there was a C-47 waiting to take me back to Siskiyou County Airport and my sweet wife Phyllis. I did hear that the game today was not pretty and still nobody cared.

The C-47 ride home was not the same as when I went down thinking about this great adventure I was on. After 48 years, I'm thankful that my mind is still functioning "sometimes".

With my flight home on Friday afternoon arriving after 4:30pm our operations offices were closed and I didn't have to report back until Monday. I was glad to get home, hug my bride and relax from my great adventure.

Monday morning was not far off and I knew that we would have to get serious about why I was there and what my duties would be. I was anxious to get started at Siskiyou County Airport.

17. Maerz 183

5. Mai

Wolkramshausen

ex decreto vom 25. Februar 1831

# CHAPTER 7

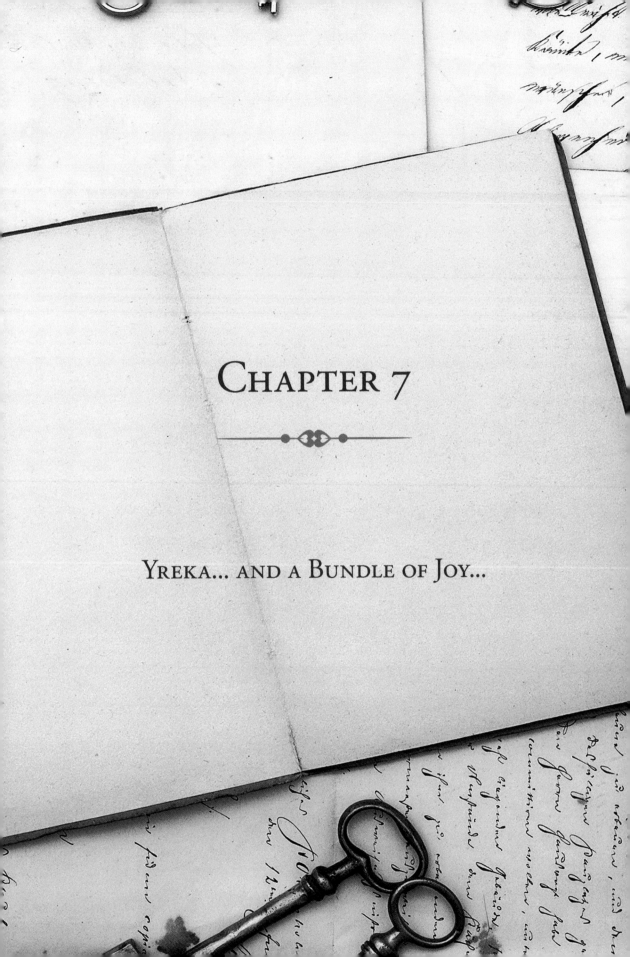

YREKA... AND A BUNDLE OF JOY...

*I*t didn't take long for Monday morning to roll around with the alarm going off at 6am. My appointment for the 2nd time was scheduled for 8am to find out why we were here at Siskiyou County Airport way up by the California-Oregon border. Was it some secret base we had with a secret mission? I would soon find out.

At 8am sharp, I met with our CO. We exchanged stories about my time at Hamilton AFB and how well our softball team did, even though we lost our last game.

When we finally got around to why we were here at the Siskiyou County Airport, I was given the following confidential information.

Hamilton AFB was the west coast base for the United States Air Defense Command. Our AirTraffic Control support group stationed at Hamilton was responsible for launching and recovering fighter jets in case of a national emergency and attack on our country.

Siskiyou County Airport was 200+ Air miles from Hamilton AFB and was designated as the primary recovery airport for damaged aircraft and problems with hung missiles.

We had a fully operational GCA (Ground Controlled Approach) facility to recover our aircraft that had been damaged. In addition we had a one story, fully operational Control Tower that was in contact with any incoming aircraft that needed our help. On the west side of our 7,500 foot runway was a fully operational FAA facility that notified us of inbound aircraft.

It was my responsibility to operate the Control Tower in a professional manner and direct landings and take-offs of all aircraft. If an aircraft was without radio communications, we were authorized to use our multi colored "light gun" to direct traffic. Green was for landing, Red was for no landing and Yellow was to use caution.

In addition to military and authorized civilian aircraft, the airport was surrounded by many farming communities that used crop dusters that had no radios and didn't use what they had. When that happened, the FAA was informed and the pilots were admonished for their actions.

The FAA gave us permission to cross the active runway and we went to the GCA Radar unit and met the guys on duty. I was not qualified to work in the GCA which was fine with me.

We then went to the Control Tower and first met the radio repair man for our detachment. He took us up one flight of stairs to the control tower that was just fifteen feet off the ground. To say the least, it was quite different than the ten story tower at my last base in Alaska.

It's hard to describe what the Control Tower looked like. It was a red and white ten foot square striped box on top of stilts with windows on all four sides. It had many radios, phones and communication equipment that rarely worked all the time.

In fact, it was a "Navy" one man control tower that was borrowed from somewhere and our Air Force radio man was lost at times on how to fix the Navy Radios.

The Tower was operated by four different controllers that rotated shifts monthly. I had the feeling that the mid-shift was going to be really boring and very dark.

With the end of our tour, I was told to report back to the base and spend the next several days training and getting use to the routine of the airport.

Hi Ho – Hi Ho, it's off to work I go.

Travel to and from the airport was only 11 miles and the country roads were great to drive on with our Big Blue Buick Wagon.

Training consisted of sitting around talking about where we both had been stationed and how we got to Siskiyou Airport. Then, from time to time, we did talk to arriving aircraft. I had to wonder, with the training and experience I had received in Alaska, why was I sent to this County Airport with very little traffic?

Were they letting me relax and enjoy myself before they sent me someplace that would really be tough? I finally realized that someone above was looking out for me and I shouldn't question my being here and get on with my job and my family.

Things on the home front in Yreka were really beginning to shape up for the Perry's. When we got the loan to buy our furniture, we knew that both of us would have to get jobs to pay off the debt.

Phyllis, with her banking experience in Alaska, started applying with the two local banks, Bank of America and the local Scott Valley Bank not too far from where we lived.

It didn't take Scott Valley Bank long to realize the talent Phyllis had and she was hired two days after turning in her application. Scott Valley Bank, way back in 1966 was nothing like the banks of today. The tellers did everything… from being a teller, posting transactions to accounts and sending out statements, without a computer.

It was truly a "Full Service" bank and you really got to know your teller.

Phyllis had a job and we celebrated by going out to dinner at Denny's.

Now that Phyllis had a job, it was time for me to start looking for a part-time job. I had no idea where I could find a job but I knew the grocery business from being at Ralph's Markets before going in the Air Force. After seeing what my job was going to be at the airport control tower, it left me thinking there may be lots of extra time to work part-time and have no conflict with my 1st duty, The Air Force.

As I've said many times, Yreka was a very small town with many small businesses to meet the needs of the local residents. We had two Banks, one Drug store and one Grocery store, Safeway which was in a very small building and needed to expand.

I put together a short resume which included my job in the Air Force at Siskiyou Airport, my previous job in Alaska and the years I spent with Ralphs Markets in Southern California and went off to meet the manger.

His name was Mr. Gorman and for some reason, we hit it off from the start. I let him know I was only looking for a part-time job and didn't live far from his store. He let me know that there were Air Force people who had worked for him in the past and they all did a good job... I assured him I would do a great Job and he asked when I could start.

Prior to applying for the job, I had to plan when I could work since I was on rotating shifts at the airport. I knew that when I worked the day shift from 8am to 4pm, I could work in the evening after 6pm. When I was on swing-shift, I could work in the mornings and afternoon till 2pm and when I worked the midnight shift I could work after 10am during the day.

With all my preparation prior to coming to see him, I guess he knew I was serious about the job and said he would put me on the schedule for next week. Wow, now I had a second job and it was time to celebrate again.

Yes, we went out to Denny's for dinner again.

# PUTTING OUR EFFORTS INTO ACTION!!!!

Since our mid-June arrival here in Yreka, we have become a real team and honestly "Worked our Butts Off" to adapt to the challenges we have met head on.

Here's a short summary of what we accomplished in less than 30 days.

- ✔ Didn't like the 1st apartment our contact found and couldn't get our money back?

- ✔ Found the perfect apartment for us two blocks up the street, paid our second rent and moved right in.

- ✔ Realized that we had no furniture, went to the Bank and got our loan approved in two days.

- ✔ Went to the furniture store where we had found most of what we needed and they delivered the same day.

- ✔ Started looking for jobs to pay the loans back. Phyllis got her full-time job at Scott Valley Bank in two days.

- ✔ The next week, I found a part-time job at Safeway that would work around my duties in the Air Force.

When all was said and done, we were delighted with the results and had been "Truly Blessed".

**Little did we know that it was going to get even better?**

When you're younger, it seems to be easier to focus on the goals you want to accomplish and nothing had better get in your way. We had spent so much time getting settled in a new town with new jobs and new friends, there seemed to be no time to think around the corner and take a look at what's ahead.

One Saturday night, we were watching television when Phyllis, out of the clear blue sky asked me a simple question that at first took my breath away and momentarily turned me white as a sheet.

**Phyllis simply asked what I thought about having a baby?.** I told her that I didn't want to have a baby myself and if we wanted to have one together, I was all for that and how soon could we get started?

We both agreed our efforts and results had been great since we arrived and now was the right time to bring a new baby into the world that we could love and grow with in our married life. After all, we had been married over two years and we were beginning to get those questions asking about Grandchildren from our parents.

Once we realized that when the baby was born, we would be having all those friends and relatives coming up to visit and where would we putting them with only two bedrooms. You know how those things happen, you think about one thing and something new is added and all the sudden you're looking in the Yreka Gazette for houses to rent.

We were off to the races having a baby. Phyllis was off to Scott Valley Bank and I was off to my Air Force job sitting in that red & white control tower on stilts waiting for airplanes that only showed up once in a while.

The busiest time of the year was during the summer when forest fires seemed to be starting on a regular basis. Siskiyou County Airport was also the home base for the Northern California Fire Fighting Aircraft and their Borate fire suppression material. Their aircraft included B-24's, B-25's and P-38's. Most of those aircraft had very poor radios and many times showed up on final approach without warning.

We had a total of 5 airplanes equipped to drop "PINK" Fire Suppression Borate material on the forest fires at a very low altitude. Before I went in the Air Force, I had seen the movies where the planes had dropped the borate on several fires and then returned to their home base to load up and return to the fire.

The real action for me was when the planes were in-bound to the airport and had called in to the FAA with their estimated arrival times and the FAA then notified me.

Don't forget that these aircraft were old, slow and had poor radios to communicate with our control tower. In addition, if any of their borate did not get dropped, they couldn't land and had to drop it somewhere close to the airport because the pink liquid would harden if left in the aircraft.

To the northwest of the airport there was a small hill which was 300 feet high that some said it had the shape of a Christmas tree. Others said it looked like something else.

When the planes were inbound and called in for landing instructions, we asked if they had Borate that they needed to dump? If they did, they were given permission to empty their tanks on the small hill. As the fires continued down south, and the planes continued their flights, there always seemed to be excess "Pink" Borate to be dropped. By the end of summer, our pink Christmas tree or whatever you wanted to call it was quite a site and many residents from Yreka would come out to see just how pink is was.

Working the day shift during the fire season made for an exciting time when the planes with no radios were coming in for landings and we had to use our light guns to communicate with the pilots.

One day as we were landing the planes, I even had a "Crop Duster" land on a taxiway next to the tower and ask if he could use the bathroom!!!!!

Back in town.

During the summer we met some great people though Phyllis's work, the friends I made in the Air Force and at Safeway. The town continued to grow on us and the scenery was spectacular with Mount Shasta less than 15 miles away.

I actually had time to play golf and getting up early in the morning meant that it was just me on the course. I even remember walking in the rain to play 18 holes, believe it or not. .

We had friends, Joan and Pinkey come up from Southern California in their camper truck and we went fishing and hunting while they were here and had a great time. We always visited them when we went back to Southern California.

My full-time Air Force job was working out great and I would change shifts with guys who had families at home and take their midnight shifts. The best part of the midnight shifts was that I could sleep in the tower and if a plane did come in, the FAA across the runway, would call to wake me up for their landing.

The Tower was a great place to sleep with the radios keeping the temperatures in the mid 80's all night long. When it was time to change shifts I was awake and having my coffee when they arrived.

With the drive home to Yreka only 11 miles, I was able to get home, take a shower, put on my shirt and tie and be to work by 10am... that was great.

When I first started at Safeway, some of the guys thought I was trying to take their jobs away. When I told them that I was only part time, that made a big difference and we all got along great.

When I went to work on mid-shift and wasn't sleepy, I got interested in photography because Mount Shasta just 15 miles off the south end of our runway was so beautiful in the dark with the moon shining on it... I could almost hear the mountian calling, please take my picture... So I did and I did and I did. I lost track of how many pictures I had taken.

We had a great camera that I thought was taking great pictures but I always had to wait for them to be developed and it seemed to take forever. One time when I was at the photo shop, I asked the owner where I might find some used photo developing equipment that I could learn to use to develop my pictures.

Much to my surprise, he said that he had some old equipment that he was looking to find a good home for and asked if I might be the guy? I felt my heart skip a beat and asked what kind of equipment it was and how much would it cost me. Again, I couldn't believe that he said I could just have it and I should come by next week when he would have a chance to round it all up. I must have thanked him ten times, said good bye till next week and hurried home to tell Phyllis. She said that it was great, and then asked where would we put it?

I said, if we get a house, maybe it will have a basement where I could do the photo developing.

The hunt for a house was on and we were looking for a place that was in town, had at least 3 bedrooms for our friends and families that would be coming, enough room to put all our furniture in and maybe a dining room where we could eat.

If we were really lucky, maybe it would even have a garage which we hadn't seen for years. We also thought about what kind of neighbors we would have.

We got the word out quickly to our ever growing circle of friends and within a week, we were in and out of lots of homes that just didn't feel right.

Our apartment was across the street from the Volunteer Fire Department in town and one afternoon we decided to go take a look and see how it operated. While we were there, the Fire Alarm went off, and all the volunteers that were working close to the station, drove to the station and jumped on the fire trucks and were off to the fire.

It got really crazy at the station with everyone running around and jumping of the fire trucks. We stayed out of the way and decided we would go back when there wasn't a fire in town.

About a week later we went back to the Fire Department and met a few volunteers manning the station. They were very friendly and showed us around. Most of them had lived in Yreka their entire life.

We talked about my Air Force Job and what I did. They asked many questions about being in the control tower.

During our conversation, I asked them if they knew of any homes that were up for rent and they thought there was one on Jackson Street not far away and it was owned by one of the guys in the fire department.

After we went back to our apartment, it didn't take us anytime to jump in the car and off to Jackson Street we went. There was a sign out front that had a phone number to call and we quickly wrote it down.

We waited till the end of the day to call in hopes of getting a look at the house and what the rent was. After 6pm we called the number on the sign and talked to the owner Mr. Quigley and he agreed to show us the house that evening.

We met Mr. Quigley at 7pm and took a good look at the entire house. It looked great and even had a basement and a garage.

To say the least, we were excited and only had one small problem, I didn't get paid for another two weeks and would he hold the house for us. Our blessings continued when he said **yes**.

The next two weeks really seemed to drag as I waited for my Air Force Check to be deposited. It didn't take us long to pack and we were ready to move in three days. Moving weekend arrived and we were up early to get started. We had been blessed with meeting many new people since our arrival and everyone wanted to help with the move. It was great having the help when it got to getting the furniture down the stairs.

Before we knew it, we were "All In" at our new home on Jackson Street and could finally sit down, take a deep breath and begin to figure out where everything was suppose to go.

With all the commotion of moving in, it didn't take us long to meet our new neighbors, Bob & Addeen Schultz and their children. We then discovered that we had moved into a house between several Family Members living on both sides of us and they couldn't do enough to make us feel right at home.

Our friendship with Bob & Addeen grew rapidly and we became part of the family on Jackson Street. Bob worked for John Deere repairing tractors and farm equipment and Addeen was a teacher at the local elementary school. All the men were part of the Volunteer Fire Department and their Fire Alert Radios would go off at all times during the night which we go use to.

We always seemed to be invited to the many family gathering they had and we even went up to their mountain cabin and enjoyed a Thanksgiving Dinner.

Once again, we had been Blessed with this move and decided to stay at home for dinner and enjoy our new home.

That decision changed quickly when we decided to stop by the only ice cream store in town that packed any flavor of ice cream you could think of? We got cones of our usual flavors, Rocky Road and Chocolate Chip. Phyllis asked me if I had ever had "Chocolate Mint Chip" Ice cream. When I said no, she thought it would be great if they could make that kind of ice cream for us and we would have it on her upcoming birthday.

Fortunately for me, I took the hint and returned to the Ice Cream store the next day and ordered custom made "Chocolate Mint Chip" ice cream that I would surprise her with on her upcoming birthday. On her birthday, I secretly picked up the ice cream on my way home from work and made a big deal out of getting her favorite, "Chocolate Mint Chip" ice cream. Boy, was she excited about what I had done and couldn't wait to have some.

That all changed when she opened the ice cream carton and said "What kind of ice cream is this"? I told her what I had done and what I told the ice cream maker. After a few tears and laughter, she told me how the "Mint Chocolate Chip" ice cream should have been made. Our Chocolate ice cream had been made with "Peppermint Chips" crushed up in the ice cream and it wasn't good enough to eat... so we didn't.

It's amazing how time seems to fly by when you're having fun. We had arrived in the small town of Yreka, California in June 1966 and asked ourselves why were we here? We thought by getting back to any part of California, we would almost be home.

It was almost fall now with the leaves and landscape changing daily and our thoughts about this small town seemed to get better with every passing day.

We had been here just four months, accomplished a ton of things and been truly blessed in the process.

Phyllis's job at Scott Valley Bank was going well, My Air Force job at Siskiyou County Airport was turning out great with plenty of time to work for Safeway part-time.

We were renting our 1st home next to some great families on Jackson Street and we were settling in for the coming winter. We even joined a Bowling League that we did once a week... What could be better?

**And then it happened,** Phyllis announced that she was pregnant with our 1st child and I had better paint the extra bedroom because the baby would be here in June of 1967 which was only 9 months away. Yes, I cried a bunch.

She then informed me that the girls at the bank had told her that she couldn't go to the hospital here in Yreka because they didn't have all the new equipment if there were complications during delivery.

I thought since the baby's arrival was 9 months away, there wasn't a great rush... Wrong!!!! The search started immediately with our Jackson Street neighbors and the medical contacts they may have in Medford, Oregon.

We had no problem getting an early start finding a doctor in Medford. The problem I envisioned was trying to get my pregnant wife to Medford, Oregon and crossing the Siskiyou mountain range in our Big Blue Buick Station Wagon in the dead of winter with snow everywhere.

Phyllis had no problem in reminding me the baby wasn't due till June and it would be in the summer. Da. It's amazing how the mind can get confused when you're going to be a dad for the first time.

With the help of many friends who had their children in Medford Oregon, Dr. McLaughlin was highly recommended and we were comfortable with being his patient. Our monthly visits became part of our routine and the 100 miles round trip to Medford seemed shorter as the months passed. With each Doctors visit, we were told that everything was right on schedule.

With the new baby's arrival getting closer and closer, we decided to take one last trip to good old Southern California for another load of wedding gifts that we hadn't seen in years.

The trip down and back was different this time since Phyllis's doctor told us that it would be best for the new baby on the way if she didn't sit in the car for extended periods of time and insisted we stop every hour and let Phyllis out to walk around.

Since there was no arguing with the doctor, this close to delivery, we stopped, and stopped, and stopped again which added three hours to the trip back home.

This time, we were on a schedule to put us home for a good night's rest before we had to go to Medford, Oregon for Phyllis's check-up with her doctor.

When we got to Redding, California, the weather was closing in with snow in the forecast for the Siskiyou Mountains. If we didn't have the Medford appointment the next day, we would have stayed overnight and started home the next morning.

In addition, Phyllis's pregnancy had gone very well and was coming to the end in just three weeks and there was no way that we were going to miss her appointment the next morning.

After a short discussion and a few tears, we checked the map and found it was 97 miles and 1 & ½ hours to get us home. We made the decision to "Press-On" and headed back to Interstate 5.

What we found as we turned north on the highway was not a pretty site. The forecasted snow had started building up on the highway and we were committed to driving in snow tracks the entire way back to Yreka which took 3 hours till we were home.

Have you ever been on a long trip and looked forward to getting home? What a relief it was to see our Home Sweet Home.

Time seemed to fly by as we got closer to Phyllis's delivery date, which was still three weeks away. Phyllis woke up one morning and suggested to go see Doctor McLaughland for a quick check up.

When the doctor had finished his examination, we were told that Phyllis was in the early stages of labor and she needed to check into Rogue Valley Memorial Hospital.

We weren't prepared for his decision and hadn't packed a bag for the hospital. We got Phyllis all checked in when the doctor arrived and told us that it would probably be 10 hours until the baby arrived.

When I recovered from the shock of what was about to happen, we realized that we needed to tell the people at Scott Valley Bank that Phyllis was in labor in the hospital. Then, there was my Air Force job and I needed to let them know that I wouldn't be there for my shift.

With the doctor's assurance that it would be 10 hours before delivery, Phyllis let me know that I had to drive to Yreka and give them the good news.

Then... I was told that I had to go home and pack a bag for her clothes and clothes for the new baby.

And... while I was doing that I might as well do a load laundry for when she got home... (True).

If I'm remembering correctly, I was told to jump into our Big Blue Buick Station Wagon, drive back to Yreka, let everyone know what was happening, do my assigned jobs then jump back in the car and come back to Medford, Oregon to be with her and the little one.

To this day, I still don't know why I just didn't call everyone and stay with Phyllis for the next 10 hours.

When I did arrive back at the hospital in 4 ½ hours, I walked in the front door and coming towards me was our doctor. He said hi, then proceeded to tell me that I must have heard. I said

What?. He said, you are the proud father of a beautiful baby girl!... Which just let the old tear ducks cut loose and I was finally a Dad !!!!

Then, he proceeded to tell me that Phyllis and our new daughter were doing great... and he was sorry that I wasn't there or I could have come into the delivery room to be with Phyllis. If I had known that, I would have never left the hospital... Who cares about "Clean Clothes" when you're becoming a New Father...

**Our Precious daughter Melody Ann Perry was born on June 12th 1967 at 4:51pm and weighed in at a hefty 5 pounds, 6 ounces because she was three weeks early.**

Phyllis and I agreed on the first name of Melody for two different reasons; a Song and a cute cowgirl Phyllis saw on the TV. The Ann part of her name was from Phyllis and the Perry name came from me.

From the time we announced the arrival of our new daughter Melody to the world, things began to get a little crazy here in Yreka. All our friends were coming over to take a look at our new baby girl and tell us how adorable she was.

Phyllis stopped working at the bank when Melody arrived and became a full-time Mom. The girls at the bank had been planning a shower for Phyllis and when she got home from the hospital they all decided to come over and have the shower anyway which turned into a big event. I think they even asked me to leave and not get in the way.

Six weeks after Melody was born, we went back to Medford for Phyllis and Melody's 1st check up with Dr. McLaughlin. Both girls were doing fine and Melody was continuing to gain weight. The Perry's were beginning to be a family and I looked forward to what was ahead of us.

With everything that was happening around us so quickly, I realized that I was now the only "Bread Winner" for our family and put myself in high gear to keep things running smoothly.

My Air Force job at Siskiyou County Airport was running smoothly and my hours at Safeway were being increased to help pay the bills. I was even considering staying in Yreka when I got discharged in February 1968 and working for Safeway.

I'm not sure how we survived all of the visitors that came and went during the summer months including both sets of parents, family members and friends from sunny Southern California. We were glad to see them come and see them go.

With fall approaching, it was time to go back to Medford for another visit with Dr. McLaughlin. We were looking forward to the visit to show off Melody and how great she was doing.

When the Doctor was checking Melody's arms and legs, he discovered that her right leg and foot were turning inward and something must be done to correct the problem immediately. We were given the address of an orthopedic shoe store and told to contact them to secure the proper fitting brace for her leg.

Hard sole shoes were purchased and then attached to the brace to help change the direction of her leg and foot. We were told that the brace must be worn when Melody was in her bed at night.

To Say the least, Melody was not happy with the shoes and brace that Phyllis had to put on her little legs and feet.

Melody's room was a little nursery at the back of the house that was just six feet from our bedroom. Every evening when it was bedtime for Melody we had to put the orthopedic brace and the shoes on her tiny feet and adjust the right shoe to face outward. It was not a pretty sight and it broke our hearts every time.

# My Best Air Force Decision
# The Reason I Said NO!!!

It was the beginning of winter in Yreka with new snow on Mount Shasta. My Air Force job was going well and my part-time work at Safeway was helping pay the extra bills for the three of us. Phyllis was happy at home taking care of our daughter Melody who was growing rapidly.

We had been in Yreka since June 1966 and were scheduled to get out of the service in February 1968 and the plan was to move back to Southern California. My part-time 20 hours a week job at Safeway had turned into 30 hours and I was now the boss of the evening shifts.

I did consider staying in the Grocery business at Safeway and transferring to Southern California until I was told I couldn't transfer to another division and I would have to start over again. That ended my thoughts very quickly.

The first part of December, I was asked if I would consider re-enlisting for another 4 years and I would be promoted to Staff Sergeant with a raise in pay.

Phyllis and I discussed what had been offered and were prepared to say no when I received a call from my Commanding Officer informing me that I had been promoted to Staff Sergeant effective immediately.

That phone call really sealed the deal. As a Staff Sergeant, the Air Force had to move me and my family back to our "Home of Record" and that just happened to be "Southern California". We were truly "Blessed Again".

After I was out of the Air Force, we did find out from friends still in the service, that the Air Traffic Controllers that went to Vietnam, were dropped behind enemy lines as "Forward Air Controllers" and many of them did not return...

*Our bundle of joy!*
*In my heart there rings a Melody!*
*Our first child.*

Bill, Phyllis & Melody

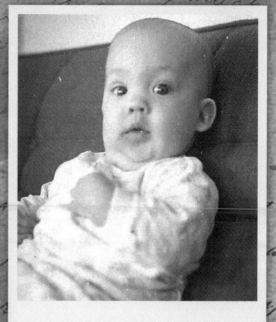

Melody 4 Months Old

Family Church Photo

Dear Miss Lloyd

Can you take a sitting for the head at the R—A— on Tuesday next? If so will you be at the studios at a quarter before ten.

Yours truly
D. W. Wainewright

...menn Stoll, Platz...

...Wolkramshaußen

17. Maerz 183.
5. Mai

...von Wurmb'schen Gütern abgeschrieben...

...ex decreto vom 25. Februar 1834 denen...

...zugeschrieben.

# CHAPTER 8

"Home Sweet Home"(?)

February 1968

*I*t didn't take long to crank things up for our return to Sunny Southern California. My Air Force service had come to an end and it was full-speed ahead to get packed and ready to finally Get Home. With my new promotion to Staff Sergeant, the Air Force was now committed to moving the Perry family back to our "Home of Record" which was Los Angeles.

Phyllis was so excited that she could hardly sit still when we were making our plans for the move. We had no idea where we would be living and where we would store our household goods from our house here in Yreka.

We set out to plan our return trip to Los Angeles and decided that we would go through San Francisco so we could go down Highway 101 and see the places where we had stayed on our honeymoon four years ago.

To do that, we needed to cross over the Bay Bridge to get onto Highway 101. Our daughter Melody who was now 8 months old was in her bassinette on the back seat and sound asleep when we started to cross the bridge. Since I wasn't familiar with this bridge, I was diving very carefully and reading the signs that would get us on the right highway going south.

I looked in my rear-view mirror and Melody was looking back at me with a Big Smile on her face. We couldn't believe that Melody had gotten up on her knees in the bassinette without any help. Fortunately for us, we didn't panic and were just amazed at what she had done. As soon as we got across the bridge, we got off the next exit to make sure that we were all ok.

It must be noted, that in 1968, there were seat belts for adults and no car seats or restraints for children. I don't want to think what might have happened if we had gotten in an accident.

We had no problem getting out of the traffic and onto Highway 101 going south. We had planned to drive all the way to Santa Barbara, then changed our minds when we checked the mileage and found out it was over 300 miles. We did make it to San Louis Obispo which was only 200 miles and called it an "Eventful Day"... which it was.

We all got a good night's sleep and were up early, had a quick breakfast and were determined to make it to Los Angeles, only 190 miles away.

It wasn't easy to do but we got on the road by 9am and had our Big Blue Buick Station Wagon take us home to Huntington Park and South Gate.

Our family reunion with both sets of parents included all the hugging and tears that we had waited for and enjoyed every minute of our return.

That being done, we decided that we would stay with my parents in Huntington Park to start and see how that worked out as we looked for an apartment we could breathe in and room for all our furniture that was to arrive in two weeks from Yreka.

Fortunately, we quickly found a two bedroom apartment in Huntington Park and contacted the moving company with the address to deliver the furniture.

With Phyllis and Melody staying at my parent's house, it was time to start looking for a new job.

Step number one was to contact the Federal Aviation Agency and see what had to be done to work as an Air Traffic controller here in Southern California. That didn't take long and I was scheduled for a battery of tests to see if I was qualified.

I must have passed the tests with flying colors because it didn't take long before I was contacted to come in for an interview. The interview went well until we got to the part when I was told the positions there were available. I was offered a job in the Air Traffic Control Center in Palmdale, California and I would be trained as a radar operator for aircraft coming into Southern California. Re-training was not in my plan since I had been a Tower controller for 4 years.

Without putting my foot in my mouth, I asked if I could visit the Palmdale location with my wife Phyllis and consider the opportunity. He agreed and the next day, Phyllis and I were off to Palmdale. It was an hour's drive from Los Angeles when we got off the freeway we stopped at a local drug store to ask for directions. When we got out of the car, there was a hot wind blowing all around us.

Phyllis went inside and asked one of the clerks if the wind always blew like this in Palmdale? The clerk laughed and then told Phyllis that "She should see it, when the wind really blows".

What the clerk didn't know was that Phyllis, from time to time would put her hair into what was called a Beehive style which she was wearing that day and the Beehive was "Leaning to the side" and looked like it was going to fall over.

When Phyllis came back to the car, she simply said to me, "If you're going to work here, you're coming by yourself". I guess she meant, look for another job.

When we got back to my parents house and shared the story of the Beehive, we all had a good chuckle and I decided to look for another job.

My Mom & Dad mentioned that we had a few relatives here in Los Angeles and maybe he had some contacts that would help. My dad asked if I had a resume, and if not, I should make one just in case I did get an interview...

I had to ask what a resume was and was embarrassed when he told me it was a story of where I had worked before I went in the Air Force and what I was doing just before I got out. That seemed easy and it didn't take long before the resume was done and was approved by my dad.

My dad, Charlie Perry, did some calling around to our relatives in Glendale who my parents had lived with when we first came to California. It must have been one those "Blessing Things" because he found out that one of my uncles was a sugar broker for C&H Sugar and may have a contact with the Shasta beverage company.

I spoke briefly with my uncle on the phone and he said he would be happy to contact the sales manager and see if I could get an interview with him the following week?

I received a phone call Monday afternoon and it was the Sales Manager at Shasta. We had a brief conversation on the phone which lead to an interview on Thursday morning at 10am.

With my resume in hand, I met with the Sales Manager and we discussed my experience in dealing with people and had I ever done "Selling" products? I told him of my background when I worked for Ralphs Markets and how I was always selling when I worked as a clerk. We then talked about my Air Force job and the pressure of working in a control tower.

I must have said all the right things and at the end of the interview, he offered me a Sales job at Shasta and how soon could I start. What was even better, I would get paid $700.00 a month salary and a company car that I could even use on weekends with my family. Of course I said yes to the job and the Perry's were off to the races with the future looking bright.

Phyllis drove me to pick up my company car on Monday morning and I stayed for a sales meeting and met the guys on the sales team. The territory where I was to work was not far from my parent's house which was great. They loaded the car with soda pop and sales material and I was officially "Off to the Races" in a new career.

Since I now had a new job with an income, Phyllis went looking for a position with one of the local banks and landed a job with City National Bank in South Gate not far from our parents homes. Phyllis was able to drop Melody off at her parent's house and was well taken care by her Grandma & Grandpa, Don & Sadie Brouard who were both retired and anxious to share their love with our new daughter.

With Melody at Don & Sadie's during the week, it was a great place for my parents, Charlie and Wilma Perry to spend time with Melody and watch her grow.

Sometimes, when Phyllis and I got done working during the day, we would end up at the Brouards to have dinner and enjoy our new daughter.

My initial job was to contact the Grocery and Drug stores and gain new distribution on Shasta Sodas that were ordered from their distributor Certified Grocers. Many stores already carried Shasta and getting a new flavor on the shelf was my job.

Shortly after I joined Shasta, we launched a new Draft Root Beer flavor that was really great. To get the product into the stores, I loaded up the ice chest in my car with lots of Root Beer and took ice cold samples into every store. The results were amazing with almost every store ordering the new Root Beer and some even asking if I would build a display when their order arrived. For some reason, the other sales people didn't think about the cold Root Beer samples and I won several contests..

With our daughter Melody growing rapidly we made the decision to find a house we could rent in an area close to our parents that would help when we needed someone to babysit. We started looking and were amazed when we found a home around the corner from where my mother was living and close to both of our parents.

We met with the owner. She showed us the home and it was perfect. With three bedrooms, a big backyard, office space for me, and a garage where I could store all my samples, we rented the house on the spot and started making our plans for moving in. Finding friends to help us didn't take long and it was great to be home.

I worked for Shasta Beverages a total of twenty months. During that time, Phyllis found out she was pregnant with our second child and was due in June, 1969.

We had been blessed with finding a home in South Gate so close to our parents. With the three bedrooms we now had, there was room for our family to grow.

Phyllis's OBGYN's office was in Lynwood, California, across the street from the hospital, and not far from where we were living.

When we were getting close to her delivery date, we went to the doctor's office for a quick check up to make sure everything was okay.

The doctor asked Phyllis, "How long have you been in labor?" Phyllis said "What labor? I feel fine."

The Doctor then said, "Leave the office right now and go across the street to the hospital and admit yourself immediately, your baby is 'On Its Way'".

Phyllis not following any directions as she was told, wanted to go to a coffee shop up the street and get something to eat and then we would go to the hospital.

This was not my plan! My plan was to do what the doctor had said, got to the hospital and I would buy her a snack. Then if something happened, at least we were at the hospital and the right people could take care of her.

I sure felt better as we entered the hospital, checked in, and got Phyllis in a wheel chair and they were off to Delivery. Way back in 1969, getting my wife to the hospital was my job and everything after that was their job.

There was no "show and tell" for the Dads in the delivery room. It was "not allowed".

I was sent to the waiting room to wait. The waiting room took me back a few years when Melody was born in Oregon and I could have been in the delivery room if I had been there… but I was NOT!

Not being in the delivery room for Cynthia's birth made two opportunities I missed. If we were blessed with a third child, I would be in the delivery room for sure!

The Lord had to know I would need another daughter in my life and He delivered her right on time. Cynthia Diane Perry was born on Wednesday, June 11th, 1969 at 10:21pm and she weighed 6 pounds, 12 ounces and was 21 inches tall.

Phyllis said the doctor even took a phone call from his daughter during the delivery and told the nurse he would call her back!!!!

Cynthia's names come from:

Cynthia… means "Moon Goddess" (Greek)

Diane… means "Pure Goddess of the Moon" (Italian)

Perry… Yea, I got in there at last.

With the birth of Cynthia, our family had grown to four and we were again thankful that we had found a home in South Gate so close to our parents.

To this day, I wake up each morning thanking the Lord for the blessings he has given us.

I continued working for Shasta in the San Fernando Valley and daily got into the "Reverse Commute Game" five days a week. As the weeks and months rolled along, selling soda pop became more of a chore than a pleasure.

# A New Opportunity...

One afternoon, I was calling on a Drug store in the valley and I met another salesman who worked for Kimberly-Clark Corporation. In our conversation, he asked me if was happy working for Shasta and would I consider applying for a job at Kimberly-Clark? He said that there was a contest on and If I got hired, he would get $100.00

I took his card with me and told him I would talk it over with my wife Phyllis. As I drove home in the "Reverse Commute" traffic, I thought about what it might be like to get out of the Soda Pop Business and work for a big company like Kimberly-Clark selling paper products like Kleenex.

I have to admit, by the time I got home, I had made up my mind to apply for the job if Phyllis and I agreed. When we talked it over and considered my potential with a larger company like Kimberly-Clark, we made the decision that it was the right thing to do.

The next morning I called the Kimberly-Clark sales person and asked how I would apply for the job. He gave me the phone number of his direct boss who was the Manager of the Drug/Mass Merchandiser Division.

The next day, I called the Division Manager and told him of my brief meeting with one of his sales representatives in the valley. He told me that he had talked to his sales person and he would like to meet me for an interview.

Kimberly-Clarks offices were in Fullerton, California and we setup an interview for the following Monday. I spent many hours over the weekend visiting stores and finding out about all the products that were made. Their products included Kotex Feminine Hygiene products and I had a lot to learn.

I met Cliff, the Division Manager, Monday morning. I had revised and added my sales experience with Shasta Beverages to the resume which brought me up to date. We met for an hour and talked about my grocery experience with Ralphs Markets and my Air Force job as an Air Traffic Controller.

I was introduced to the Regional Sales Manager and staff in the offices. Cliff and I then went to lunch, discussed what my responsibilities would be in the Non-Food Division and the territory he was looking for help in was the San Fernando Valley. By the end of lunch, Cliff had offered me a new job with Kimberly-Clark Corporation which included more money and a newer car. Yes, I did ACCEPT !

I started working for Kimberly-Clark in January, 1970, I started my new job in our Non-Foods and Mass Merchandiser Division. I spent the first two weeks learning all about the 40+ products that I would be selling which included Feminine Hygiene products like Kotex and Tampons which were all new to me. I knew that Phyllis would be happy with all the free samples.

The next two weeks I worked with several of the guys in our division, going on sales calls and merchandising our products in the stores. I don't ever remember being embarrassed with the products I was selling.

When I took the job, I knew I would be working in the San Fernando Valley and I spent several days mapping out where the drug stores and Mass Merchandiser accounts were located. I was glad that I had spent the time with Shasta Beverages and it was easy getting around when making calls on the retailers.

After working for the company for only 30 days, I was told that we were all flying to San Francisco for a big meeting and we were staying at the Mark Hopkins Hotel. The meeting was designed to launch our "Spring to the Selling Seventies" campaign. This was the first time I had ever been to a Big Meeting by a Major Corporation. I was so excited that I couldn't sit still.

Everything that was done was first class, When we got to our rooms, every pillow case said "Spring to the Selling 70's" and we were told to take the pillow cases home with us and that there would be more by the time the meeting was over.

There was no question in my mind that I had "Done the Right Thing" coming to work for Kimberly-Clark and now was my time to prove what I was capable of. Our meeting was filled with all the sales force on the West Coast and all the Product Managers from the home office in Neenah, Wisconsin. I had never met so many important people in my life and I was anxious to meet as many of them as I could.

During our meetings, we were told that Kimberly-Clark would be launching a New Line of Disposable Diapers call "Kimbies" and we were going right after Proctor & Gamble. The sales people at the meeting "Went Crazy" and couldn't wait to get started. We were also launching new packaging for our Kleenex 280 count box and it would have multi-colors of Kleenex in the same box.

Finishing the meeting and getting on the plane to go home had to be done if we were going to accomplish the objectives the meeting had set for us in our marketing areas.

When I started with Kimberly-Clark Corporation, our sales staff consisted of 5 sales people who knew each other and had worked together for years and one "New Guy", that was me. Stepping into a group of sales people that I didn't know wasn't easy.

Here I was, the new guy who wanted to learn everything I could about our company and products going to meetings with guys that had been around for some time and were content with doing their job and leaving it behind each day when they went home.

That was not Bill Perry and it didn't take long for my boss Cliff to see that I had a talent to get the jobs done and make our business grow.

In January, 1971, we were still living in South Gate and I was still driving the "Reverse Commute" every day to get to the valley and then home again. Melody was growing like a beautiful flower and our future was coming together nicely.

One evening, after Melody and Cynthia had gone to bed, Phyllis said she had something important to tell me. She was very serious when she told me she was pregnant again and the baby was due in October. I can still remember the tears of joy rushing into my eyes and my Kleenex. My mind immediately said to me… maybe we will have that son you always wanted? …and prayed for?

I didn't sleep well that night with all those thoughts running through my mind. What name shall we give him? Will he be healthy and happy?

Time flew by and Timothy Charles Perry arrived on October 15th, 1971. He weighed 7 pounds and was 18 ½ inches tall and looked just like his dad… all wrinkled up.

This time, the delivery of our baby was going to be different than anything I had ever experienced. Doctor Peterson, who delivered Cynthia, was now the head of OBGYN at Saint Francis Hospital and I asked him if I could go into the delivery room. He thought for a few seconds and said YES IF I followed all the rules.

**The rules were then explained to me:**

- ✔ I had to wear all the hospital gowns that the doctor wore.

- ✔ I could sit behind Phyllis's head and encourage her to push if I was asked.

- ✔ I couldn't ask questions…. Because it was none of my business.

- ✔ If I felt woozy and fainted, no one would pick me up until after the delivery was completed.

- ✔ I agreed to each rule as he told then to me.

**In addition, I was the 1st father that had ever been allowed in the delivery room and I "wasn't messing it up".**

From that day forward, the job in the valley took on a new meaning. I needed more time to accomplish my goals and started to consider if we should consider buying a home in the valley to cut down the time it took to get to work and get home. We had no idea where to start and I started buying newspapers all over the valley.

In one area, Woodland Hills, we found out quickly that my current income did not meet what was needed to qualify for buying a home. As our search continued we contacted a real estate agent who was willing to help us and he reminded me that I was a Veteran and we should be looking into FHA and GI Loans to finance the purchase.

That sounded great to us and we turned our search over to him. Within a few weeks, he had come up with several properties that we should look at in the Canoga Park area and we met with him the following weekend to see what he had found.

We looked at several homes with small backyards and the floor plans that just didn't work for us. On our second day of looking we found a home on Kittridge Avenue, walked through the front door and knew we were home. It had three bedrooms, two baths, a great backyard with a porch and it was in the right price range. The FHA loan papers said there was no money down, which we couldn't believe.

Yes, we signed the papers and bought the house and wanted to move in immediately. There was one small problem, the owner was living in the house and needed to move to their new home. He asked if he could have two weeks to move out and he would pay us. That sounded like a great idea and we agreed.

Now that we had agreed to buy our 1st home, we needed to get rolling and pack up all our treasures from our South Gate house and make arrangements to have them shipped and delivered to Canoga Park.

It wasn't easy to tell the owner of the house we were moving. She thanked us for taking care of the house and especially all the inside painting that we had done.

We did a great job in planning the move and it went off without a hitch.

We finally made the move to Canoga Park in May of 1972 with three great children and settled in to working in "The Valley", being home every night for dinner, getting to know the new neighbors and watching our children "Grow". What could be Better !!!!!!

Being just around the corner from my accounts and now being able to do the extra things I wanted to provide was great and the business grew rapidly. Still being the newest guy on our sales team, I knew it would take time to get my retail and corporate accounts up to where I wanted their sales to be.

With Melody turning five and getting ready to start school, Phyllis was at home raising Cindy and Timothy which were both hand-full.

We finally met Terry, Catherine and their son Matthew who lived across the street and a new friendship got off to a great start. Terry, worked for the Federal Government and made the long drive to the Port of Long Beach and back every day. Catherine was a kindergarten and first grade school teacher who always took her job very seriously.

We couldn't have been in a better neighborhood to raise our small children. Our friendship grew rapidly and we spent many happy hours together.

The days seemed to fly by and December rolled around before we knew it. Fortunately, we still had our old fake Christmas tree that came out of the box and we used it again for the 7th year... I can't remember what Christmas morning was like... except it was our 1st with all the kids running around and it was a Blessing to be a part of the celebration.

We made it through the holidays with our parents, our friends and families and looked forward to what 1973 and the future would lead us.

*Don't put off till tomorrow
what you can do today.*

Charlie Perry

*Prior Planning Permits
Perpetually Pleasing Performances*

Bill Perry

1st Easter - Bill & Melody at Bill's Parents

1st Easter at Bill's Parents House

1st Easter- Bill's Parents House

Backyard in Canoga Park

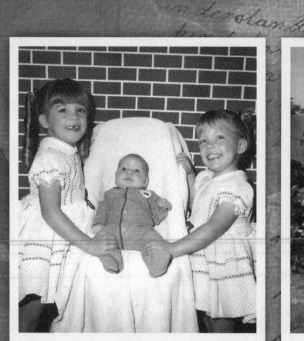

Christmas - Melody, Cindy, & Tim

Easter - Southgate House

Canoga Park - Melody, Tim, Cindy

Melody's Dance Recital

Grandma Perry and Tim

Easter at the Brouard's House

Phyllis's Parents and son John

Phyllis's Brother - Dennis and Jennifer

Phyllis & Cindy-with the Beehive

*Phyllis, Melody & Cindy*
*3 days old*

*Ten Year Class Reunion*

immer Wall, Platt
bestehen?
Jul
emann,
Wolkramshausen
17. März 183. schreiben: Fünfzig Thaler
5. Mai
rant nebauft in der Hälfte, nach dem solche
Inne Hut von Wermb'schen Güter abgeschrieben
Inne, ex decreto vom 25. Februar 1834 derken
zugeschrieben.

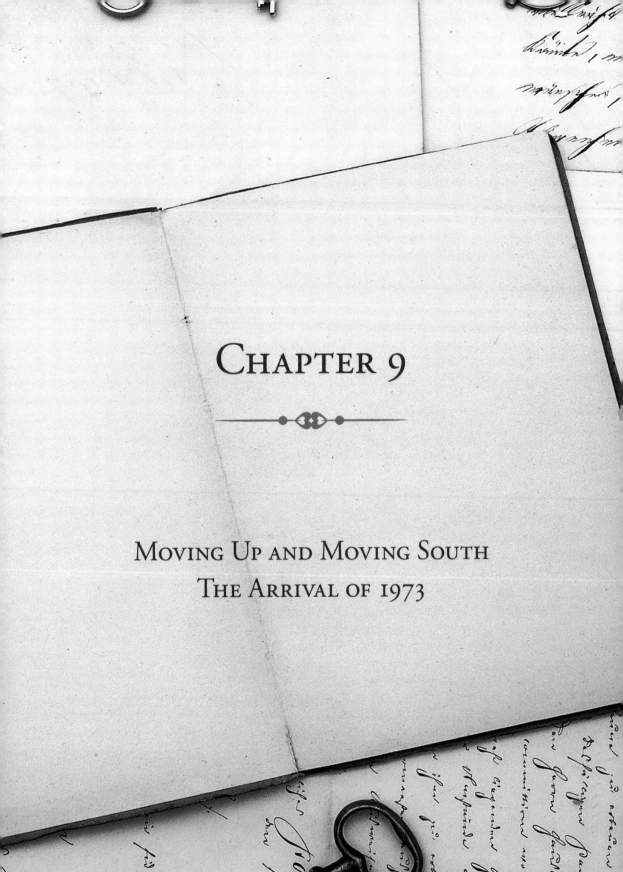

# CHAPTER 9

## MOVING UP AND MOVING SOUTH
## THE ARRIVAL OF 1973

*I*t didn't take long for the glow of Christmas and the holidays to fade into yesterday as we put the plastic tree in its box and on the shelf in the garage. The Monday following the holidays I received a call from my boss Cliff and he wanted me to come to the Fullerton Mill and Corporate Offices for a planning meeting.

I had no idea what that meant. It couldn't be bad since I had been very successful with my accounts in the San Fernando Valley. I had to get an early start to make it to Fullerton on time with all the traffic I knew would be going into the city. I knew that fifty miles in the morning traffic could be brutal and I didn't want arrive looking like I just got out of my trunk. I left home very early and made the appointment in plenty of time.

Cliff met me at the front door, asked if I wanted some coffee and we went down the hall to the cafeteria talking about our families and the weekend.

Soon after my arrival, the Regional Manager, Charlie arrived and he asked me if I had any idea why I was there? I told him that I had no idea and I hoped that my work was meeting their expectations.

I remember them both chuckling at my comment and that concerned me to a point.

It all went away when Charlie told me that I was being promoted to a "District Manager" effective immediately and he wanted me to move to San Diego and take over the operation and do there what I had been doing here.

Wow, I almost fainted with the praise they were laying on me and yes I did shed a few tears of joy.

I accepted the job with great enthusiasm and even got a great raise. I couldn't wait to get out of the offices and find a phone to call Phyllis.

When I got back to my car, I still couldn't believe what had just happened. I shed a few more tears and went looking for a phone booth.

The next thought that popped into my whirling head was "How did I get promoted ahead of 5 guys that had been with Kimberly-Clark longer than me? I must have been doing something right. I finally found a phone booth and called home "Collect".

Phyllis wanted to know if I was all right and what had happened? When I told her that I had been promoted to a District Manager and we were moving to San Diego, she was speechless and we both cried. I could hear the children in the background crying and they had no idea what was going on.

The Drive back to Canoga Park seemed to take forever and it was great to be home with the family. We had only been in our first house since May and we hoped that we could find another house quickly in San Diego.

It wasn't an easy thing to do when we told both parents that I had gotten promoted and we were moving south to San Diego, 125 miles away to be the new District Manager. All of our crying and hugging finally slowed down in a few minutes and we could tell the details of our move.

Getting started would be tough and require many trips to San Diego which meant we needed their help with taking care of the children. We knew what their answer would be in advance and they jumped on the chance while saying "Take as long as you need".

Our first priority would have to be finding a place to live and we had no idea where to begin.

Hi Ho, Hi Ho...It's off to Work I Go on another adventure !!!!!!

It was January when I had my meeting with Charlie & Cliff and we needed help in San Diego by February 1st at the latest. That meant that each week I would leave on Monday morning, check into the hotel by 10am and meet with my two sales people, John and Rudy and talk about the San Diego marketing area and the major customers we were dealing with.

When we first met, I told them that I wanted to see as many customers that I could each day and review the business we were currently doing. That went very well with both sales people and we began building our team, from the first day that we met.

The drive back home to Canoga Park was never a joy and the 100+ miles seemed to get longer each week. I knew what was going to happen when I did get home and Phyllis asked me when we were going to San Diego to find a new home so we could all be together.

I have to admit that starting the new job was my first priority and finding a house was my second. It didn't take long for the priorities were reversed, a Home and then the job. I knew I needed advise and I knew where to get it from, John & Rudy.

There was a lot on my mind as I drove down to San Diego Monday morning. I checked into the hotel as usual and met John & Rudy for our morning meeting. This Monday was different with the first thing on the agenda was, where do I find a home for Phyllis and our family.

Without any hesitation, both John & Rudy told me that I needed to look in North County where the homes were still affordable. There was a growing town called Poway which was only twenty minutes north and an easy commute.

Since I had no idea where Poway was, we changed our plans, jumped in the car and headed north. We spent several hours in Poway looking for homes, getting brochures and checking on what it would take to get into a new house. I knew that I had to take every brochure with me if I wanted to get in the house when I got home.

My welcome home was short and to the point with a quick kiss, hugging the kids and Phyllis asking, where's the brochures for the new houses? That question was followed by, are we going down this weekend, our parents will take care of the kids.

I had no choice, I guess it was time to point the company car south and head out Saturday morning, which we did. I'm sure glad I had a company Station Wagon to carry all the stuff to Grandma's, kiss the kids goodbye and head south. By the time we finally hit the road, it was early afternoon and we decided to find a motel in North County and start fresh the next morning.

We headed for Poway the next morning with all our brochures and directions on how to get to our New Dream Home?

Phyllis and I made frequent weekend trips looking for just the right home that was new with four bedrooms, a backyard and a home office for me.

On one trip down, a new development was just opening up and we dropped by to see what was being built. We looked at several homes which weren't large enough for our growing gang...and then walked into a home with a great floor plan, four bedrooms and plenty of room and we felt like we were home and decided to buy the house.

We only had one small problem, we needed a down payment of $2,500.00 and we didn't have the cash that would seal the deal.

We called home to ask for help and my Loving Mom gave us the money. I still remember her comment as she gave us the check and said "I know that your Dad, who had recently died, would have wanted to do this". It took us some time to stop the tears and crying.

With everyone's help, we had become New Homeowners and were anxious to get moved in by late February and settle down. This was my first corporate move and it seemed like it took forever till we were moved in and knew we were home.

We owned a Completed House with No lawns and No fences and we didn't care...It was Great! All of the houses around us didn't have fences or lawns either.

We met some great neighbors and decided to have a "Fence Building" project for 6 homes. Things started out well...and then went "Down-Hill" when one neighbor didn't like the way we set his posts and knocked them all over with his sledgehammer.

I think the 5 of us had a few beers and decided to re-group and went forward and finished the project in record time. I only had one small problem; I came down with pneumonia and was in bed for a week to recover.

Our "Bottom Line" was great. We were in our New Home with a fenced in backyard, no lawns, front or back. We had Great Neighbors all around us and no more driving back to Canoga Park..."What could be Better".

Our relationships with our neighbors grew rapidly and it had no other choice. All of the houses were only 10 feet apart with a fence in between and we were always talking across the fence.

Our neighbors next door were Harry & Caroline Roberts. Harry had recently retired from the phone company and was always asking us if there was something he could do for us. We spent most of our time together sitting on the patio sipping drinks.

One Friday afternoon, Harry asked me if I enjoyed football and would I like to go with him to a Chargers Game. He had season tickets somewhere around the 50 yard line and was meeting several of his friends in the parking lot for a before game tailgate party. I had to say yes and late Sunday morning we were off to the game in his Big Red Cadillac.

We met his friends in the parking lot and did what you do at tailgate gatherings before going into the game. To my surprise, his 2 seats were right on the 50 yard line.

Even more amazing, there were 2 Beers under each seat that were put there by his friends before we arrived.

The Chargers had a good team that year and by half-time we were ahead by 14 points. Harry wanted to go up the full-service bar and get a real drink. I went with him to make sure we could get back to our seats. As we lowered the seats to sit down, some else had put two more beers under our seats again...I knew that it was going to be a long afternoon. The Chargers won the game by 21 points and as we were on our way out of the stadium, his friends asked if we were going to join them for an "After-Game" drink. I mentioned to Harry that Phyllis and the kids were at home waiting for us and we decided to hit the road and go home. It was a great decision, especially when we had a hard time finding his Big Red Cadillac. I asked if I could drive, he said no and the tires squealed as we drove out of the parking lot.

Monday morning seemed to come very early and it was time to get back to the job at hand. Our sales district was coming together quickly with the three of us working as a team and looking for new business to make our numbers grow.

At our Corporate meeting several months ago in San Francisco, we were getting ready to "Go To Market" with our new Disposable Diapers called Kimbies and go "Head to Head" against Pampers.

As our launch of Kimbies drew closer, we planned who our customers would be and when we would be "On the Street" and writing "Big" orders.

Being new to the San Diego area, we wanted to go and do all the tourist things like Sea World and the San Diego Zoo as soon as possible. On one of our field trips, we drove to San Ysidro which was on the boarder of Mexico...just for the fun of it.

We were excited to go into a Foreign Country to take a look around and were "Shocked" at what we saw as we drove across the bridge getting into Tijuana. Under the bridge was a wasteland of 200 hundred "Cardboard Houses" that people were living in.

I will never forget our children in the back seat that asked, "Daddy, what are all those people doing there"? At first I was so stunned, I had no answer. They asked a second time and I told them it was where the "Poor People" lived every day...They didn't ask again and I knew we were all in shock at what they had seen.

As soon as we could, we turned the car around, drove through the shopping area and headed back to the border with a memory that I still have today.

As soon as we got across the Border, the children slowly came out of their shock and asked if we could go to McDonalds...which we did and then hurried home to the safety of our home in Poway.

I have never forgotten what I saw that day and how it would be a part of my future success with Kimberly-Clark.

We finally started receiving cases and cases of Kimbie Diapers to do our "Show and Sell" presentations to all our customers in our San Diego marketing area.

We must have done the right thing and achieved 100% distribution with all our grocery and drugstore accounts.

**For some reason, as I was driving home to Poway, I remembered our brief family trip to Tijuana, Mexico. Downtown was nothing like what we had seen "Under the Bridge", with many department stores and retailers doing business.

I had to wonder if they were doing any disposable diaper business. I did some research, made some calls and decided to go back to Tijuana and check out the stores.

Since John was the oldest member of our team, I asked him to go with me since his car was older than mine and I really didn't want to drive into a foreign country.

The boarder was only 30 miles away and we left early to avoid any traffic. We stopped to have breakfast and decided to take our ties and jackets off so we wouldn't look like salesmen.

We easily crossed the border and across the "Bridge" to downtown and visited several stores to see if anyone was selling disposable diapers. We asked a few questions in the stores and found out that Dorian's Department Stores were selling some...when they could get them.

We asked the manager of one store how we could get in contact with their offices. We found out their offices were just a few blocks away and the store manager called the office to see if the buyer was in. She was not and didn't come in till the afternoon.

The buyers name was Angelina and I got her phone number from the store manager.

John and I were both excited about the potential with these stores and we decided to get out of the country while we were ahead.

Crossing back into the United States, we were just tourists and it went smoothly...As we drove up the freeway from San Ysidro, there was a sigh of relief from both of us.

We had no idea where our efforts would take us and I looked forward to making the afternoon phone call.

I waited until 3:30pm to make the call to Dorian's and asked to speak to Angelina. There was a long pause and she finally came on the line and said hello...

For some reason, we made an "Instant Connection" within the first minute and we talked about many things before getting around to Disposable Diapers. Angelina was very interested in the potential and asked us to come back to Tijuana the next week and bring some samples of the Kimbies I agreed that we would be there on Monday afternoon after 3:30 for our appointment.

The weekend seemed to drag as I got the samples together and figured out a way to put them under the floor where the tire was stored. That worked out great and John and I were anxious for the weekend to end.

Monday afternoon we met at our "Lucky Park & Ride" north of San Ysidro to make sure we were on the same page before crossing the border. We were, and made our way to the address we had been given in Tijuana. We drove by the Steel Gated building several times not knowing if we had the right place. I rang the bell on the gate and was asked who I was and who I wanted to see. I said I had an appointment with Angelina at 3:30pm. After a few minutes, the huge Steel Gate opened and we were escorted inside.

As we walked down the driveway, I noticed there were fighting game-cocks in cages that didn't seem happy with our arrival. We picked up our walking pace and were soon at the office where we went in.

Angelina was an attractive Hispanic Lady and was glad to see us and hear all about the new Baby Diaper we were about to launch here on the West Coast.

During our conversation, Angelina informed us that Dorian's Department Stores had been doing business with the United States for years and frequently brought their trucks across the border to pick up merchandise in Southern California.

Angelina also informed us that they banked with the Bank of America in San Ysidro, and gave me the name and phone number of their banking contact.

This all seemed to be moving very quickly and as soon as we crossed the border into San Ysidro, I found the Bank of America where Dorian's did their business and I went in to speak to the contact I had been given. I told him about our contact with the buyer and their interest in our new product line of disposable diapers.

I told him who I worked for and I needed to get some financial information on Dorian's that I could pass on to my Corporate Headquarters in Fullerton, California for approval. He told me that he would have to talk with Dorian's Headquarters first before any information would be released.

The one thing that he could tell me was that Dorian's Department Stores was the Banks Largest account. I then realized how big the opportunity was with Dorian's was and I was very anxious to get started.

It seemed like it took forever to get home, to make the call to the Regional Manager in Fullerton and let him know the potential that was possible if we could get Corporate Approval from Wisconsin to do business with this customer.

I only had one small problem. In my excitement, the Corporate Offices in Fullerton were now closed and I had to wait until morning. It did give me a chance to calm down.

The next morning, I called the Fullerton offices, and spoke with the Regional Manager about all that had happened on our quick trip into Mexico. I told him about meeting with the buyer for Dorian's and her enthusiasm in wanting to purchase our new Kimbie Diapers.

I told him about our stop at the Bank of America in San Ysidro and meeting the manager who informed me that Dorian's was their number one customer and had credit lines reaching in the millions.

From the time that I submitted all the paper work that was necessary to get this new account started, the approval was received in less than two weeks and we were ready to do business when the diapers arrived in California.

The Buyer was delighted that we moved so quickly and placed her first order for (6) trailer loads of diapers when they arrived in Fullerton. So Was I...

Bringing merchandise into Tijuana was not an easy task. To solve that problem, Dorian's had three 40' trailers that were sent from Tijuana to Fullerton to pick up the diapers. When the trucks crossed the border into California, the drivers would go to the nearest truck stop and put California license plates and their trucks. It was all legal and made crossing the border much easier.

Finding a new account in a foreign country was a "Big Deal" and putting together the whole program was even bigger.

So, here I was at the age of 32, a successful sales and marketing guy who had just received his 1st corporate promotion to District Manager, moved to a new city and no one ever took me aside and explained that things were done differently by District Managers if I wanted to climb the corporate ladder to the next rung. It didn't take long to find out that my new job now included being the "Entertainment Director" when upper management came to San Diego to relax and unwind.

San Diego is less than 100 miles from Los Angeles and it didn't take me long to find out that our Regional Manager liked to come down from time to time "Blow off Steam and Relax". When he did want to come to town, he needed someone that he could relax with by playing golf, going out to dinner at his favorite restaurant and then run around town till all hours of the night.

To accomplish this great task, I was told that it was my job to reserve two hotel rooms, one for him and one for me. There was no deciding for me, it was yes, I will do that.

It was my job to be downtown early, check in for both rooms and make sure that there was Vodka, Scotch and the mixers in his room with the ice.

He always came down by airplane and I was always waiting just outside baggage claim to grab his clubs and suitcase, put them in the car and drive the half mile to the hotel and get him to his room.

When he had changed his shirt and slacks, we were off to the bar at his favorite restaurant overlooking the water and order our drinks from his favorite bar tender, Carlos.

Ordering drinks and talking about our business in San Diego consumed the next two hours while we ordered more drinks to go along with the snacks that were always served.

There was always a table waiting for us when we were "Ready to go to dinner". Sometimes, making it from the bar to the restaurant was not an easy task.

We always had the best table in the house and finally got around to ordering dinner that always came with another drink to wash the salad down.

We never missed dessert and "My Boss" always said, "Why don't we go visit Carlos for a nightcap"? Yes we did and only had one.

Then, the decision was made by "My Boss" that he wanted to go to a few "Strip Clubs" and see what was happening.

Fortunately for me, I reminded Him that we had an 8am tee time at Torrey Pines and it would be nice if we could get a fresh start. I had no idea how that always seemed to work and I left him down stairs and I went to bed.

6:30am came early in the morning and much to my surprise, he was always up and ready to play golf. We had a great day on the golf course, got back to the hotel, changed clothes and went back to visit Carlos at his favorite restaurant.

I learned quickly that this Entertainment Game was going to go on each time visitors came to my marketing area and I knew that there was no way that I could keep up their drinking and running around town all night.

I created a new plan for myself and I decided to visit our "Favorite Restaurant" and have a talk with Carlos, our favorite bar tender and tell him the problem I had running with the "Bosses" and keeping up with their drinking. He understood that I had a family that lived 10 miles up the road and they were more important than the "Bosses" who came to town.

Carlos, had the answer to my problem. He told me that I only drank screwdrivers with Vodka and orange juice which was true. His solution was easy. When we came back to the bar after dinner for a few more drinks, he would only give me "Orange Juice" with no Vodka...A Brilliant Idea !!!!!!

From that day on, I always took our visitors to the same Restaurant for dinner which was great, ended up in the bar for my "Orange Juice" cocktail and then drove them around to see the "City at Night" and took them back to our hotel so we could get an early start visiting stores or playing golf.

I managed and built the San Diego market for 2 and ½ years by working with a Great Team which continually came up with new ideas that added to our business. We won many awards for our efforts which went a long way to my growth with the company.

In November of 1975, we were attending a Regional Sales Meeting in Los Angeles when I was told that it was time for me to take on a new assignment and move back to Los Angeles as a Division Manager and take on all the responsibility of managing the Drug and Mass Merchandiser business.

My great friend Cliff, who had been with Kimberly-Clark for many years and hired me to come work for the company, was having some on-going medical problems and needed to step down to take care of himself. Cliff had recommended me for the position since I had been in the Drug/Mass Merchandiser business prior to going to San Diego.

I was amazed when I was offered the position. It wasn't a job that I could turn down and it included "Moving Up and Moving Home". I accepted the position and told no one what had happened. When I came through the front door of our home in Poway, my family was there to greet me and I broke down in tears when I told them that I had been promoted again and we were going back to Los Angeles where the Grandparents lived for Christmas.

*1973 started quickly with
a January promotion to San Diego.
Our new home was great
and our future got brighter every day.*

*A Kiss for Dad*

*Christmas -Tim, Cindy, Melody*

Cindy Sitting on the Car

Cindy's 5th Birthday

Family Christmas Card

Melody at Poway Parade

Melody's Dance Recital

House in Poway

Our Daughters

Melody, Tim, Cindy

Perry's at the Park

San Diego Lighthouse

Pool Time - Bill & Kids

Tim & Cindy Posing

Tim in Poway Park

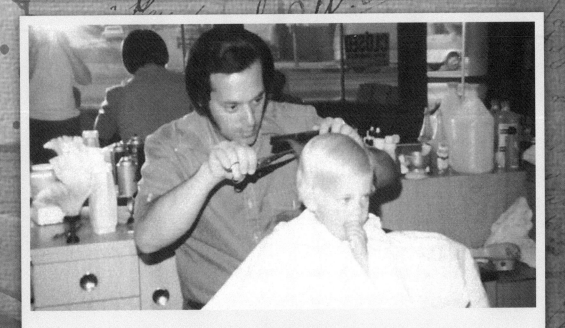

Tim's First Haircut

Wolkramshausen

17. März 183_
5. Mai

25. Februar 1834

# Chapter 10

## A Funny Thing Happened
## On My Way to Success

*P*lanning any kind of a move is no easy task. Being told in November that I had to have it done by January 1st 1976 added to the complexity of the problem with three small children anxious for the holidays to roll around with Santas Magically arriving. If I heard the question once, I heard it a hundred times; "How will Santa know where we are if we move?

Phyllis was not thrilled with the idea of a move during the holidays and came around when we invited all our parents to our new home... where ever that might be.

Our first priority was finding a new home that we could afford and hopefully somewhere close to a beach. We concentrated our efforts in the Huntington Beach area and it didn't take long to find the perfect home. The only problem we had was the family when they decided not to move and we were out of luck.

Being the creative parents that we are, it didn't take long to find our second home with High Vaulted Ceilings, three bedrooms upstairs for the kids and the master bedroom on the ground floor. This time our offer was accepted and we moved ahead full-speed to make sure Santa has his place to come.

To complete our part of Santa's Arrival, Phyllis and I secretly loaded up our station wagon with Christmas decorations and went to our new Huntington Beach home alone and decorated the empty house for Christmas which had no furniture in the house except for the Christmas tree. It looked great!!!

Back in Poway, many tears flowed when we broke the news that I had been promoted to a Division Manager and we were moving back to the Los Angeles marketing area. With the help of our great neighbors, it only took two weeks to sell our home and we were sadly able to put that piece of the puzzle behind us.

Back in Huntington Beach, we were still getting ready for Christmas. Phyllis and I were sneaking around trying to shop for gifts and then getting them assembled and wrapped for Christmas Morning.

I was pretty good with wrapping presents and was assigned the task of putting Cindy's new bike together which should have been done when the children were away...but they never left and were always asking what are you doing?

When the children were in bed, Phyllis and I moved Cindy's bike from the garage and put the box in our clothes closet so I could put it together the next day. The next day turned into a joke when the children arrived home early and here I was behind the locked bedroom door trying to finish the bike assembly.

I left the room to greet the family and forgot to lock the door. Soon after I got back to work, the door opened slowly and there was Cindy asking what I was doing? I had no choice and told her it was an exercise bike for Mom and it was a secret. She didn't say a word, just smiled, ear to ear and quietly closed the door.

I think the bike had Pink and Blue Hearts on it.

Finally, Christmas morning arrived and of course, everyone was up early and ready to go except their Mom & Dad.

Since we had invited our parents down for Christmas Day, it was a real chore to control the children's enthusiasm until they arrived and then all Chaos broke loose again.

All the effort that we put into this move at Christmas time was rewarded with the cheers and the tears that flowed that day.

Cindy got her bike, gave me a big hug and smiled again from "Ear to Ear". The Christmas of 1975 has never been forgotten.

Taking over the Division Managers Position in a Multi-Million Dollar market was not an easy task with the work that had to be done with our major customers and gaining new distribution.

Working with Cliff who I was replacing as the Division Manager went well and we spent most of first week going over the accounts that our division was responsible for and the new distribution that was needed to get us on track.

Next, we took on the task of looking at our field sales team, their years with the company, their account responsibilities and the distribution gaps that needed to be filled.

I could tell at our first meeting with the team, many of the sales people were not "Overjoyed" with having me as their new boss.

After all, I was the guy who got promoted ahead of them and they never understood why they were not considered for the San Diego Managers Job.

When I took the Managers job in San Diego, I asked myself the same question? When I started working with our team in the Los Angeles marketing area, it didn't take long to see why I was chosen; they were not totally prepared for their day's work, when they went to work.

Once we had our meeting out of the way, I started working with our sales team making presentations at the local accounts and their headquarters.

It didn't take me long to figure out who was making the most effort to move our business forward. "IT WAS ME!"

Living in Huntington Beach was great for those who loved the sun. I found that it just wasn't the best place to live and travel all over Los Angeles County to make the appointments with our Corporate Headquarters and then meet our sales people in the field for an afternoon of calling on retail accounts.

I started asking myself if I was doing this Division Manager thing the right way. Cliff and I discussed my thoughts and concerns and came to the conclusion that I was doing the right things and we needed to work on a better way to schedule working with the sales team and at Corporate Headquarters.

There wasn't a day that I wasn't out of the house by 7am, prepared to work with the sales people and make presentations at Corporate Headquarters. Most days, I usually drove into the driveway at 7pm. Cell Phones hadn't been invented yet so Phyllis had no idea where I was...and I didn't either.

As I was waiting to get on the Freeway and go 70+ miles per hour, I had to ask myself, "Where did all the people come from"? It didn't use to be like this in the "Good Old Days", just a few years ago?

Once I had said the "Good Old Days' out loud, I was amazed at how many times those words drifted into the back of my mind.

With the hectic schedule I was on, time really flew by quickly. Before I realized it, we had been in Los Angeles more than four months; Out at 7am, in at 7pm and not enjoying the freeways at 70 miles per hour.

We had a new Western Regional Manager take over the business and were looking for ways to increase our volume on the West Coast. At one of our Staff Meetings, we were told that the current Division Manager in Seattle was being moved to the Corporate Headquarters in Neenah, Wisconsin.

He asked us to think who might be able to run the Northwest Division and give him our recommendations in two weeks.

Boy, did the bells and whistles go off in my head. I knew who it should be...and it should be ME. I got home early that night and after dinner talked with Phyllis about making a move to Seattle, Washington.

To say the least, she was not pleased with the idea of leaving California again. We discussed the subject several times in the next week with no decision being made. I did explain that the Pacific Northwest was a "Stepping Stone" to the Corporate Headquarters and getting out of the "Rat Raise" in California would be great for raising the children without Millions of people day in and day out. We finally did agree the move would be best for the children and their future.

Before I saw the Regional Manager, I did two things to gain support for my move north. I had a long lunch with Cliff and explained what was going on in my "Hustle/Bustle" life since coming back to the Huge Los Angeles marketing area.

In addition I made a phone call to Mike who was the current Division Manager in Seattle and asked for his help in reaching my goal. I had worked for Mike when we were in Southern California and I knew I could count on his support.

Our recommendations were to be turned in on Monday of the next week. Instead of waiting, I made an early appointment for Saturday morning with the Regional Manager to discuss my thoughts one on one. He always said he came in on Saturday mornings and that's when we met.

Our meeting went well and he assured me that he would look into my request, consider the options and get back to me within the week.

I'm not sure what happened in their meetings and I may never know. The long week that I was prepared to wait for, turned into only three days and I became the Pacific Northwest Division Manager and we were moving to Seattle, Washington and a New Opportunity to Succeed at a much slower pace.

It's amazing what can happen when a Corporation moves quickly to fill a key position within a Region that's over 1,200 miles away. Within three weeks, I was relieved of my responsibilities in California. The house went on the market in two weeks and was sold in three weeks. The moving company was on our door step and anxious to set a date for the move.

If you're wondering what I was doing all that time, I was catching my first flight to Seattle from LAX to assume the responsibility of the Division, meet the staff in the local marketing area and look for a home for my family. Was I busy?...YES !

Was I excited about the New Opportunity?...YES !

# The "Bottom Line"

What had happened to Bill Perry was simple. I had returned to Southern California at the young age of 35 to do whatever it took to be successful and give my family a great life in Sunny California. What I found was a place that had grown and changed so fast while we were gone, I was at a loss to keep up with the progress.

What I had forgotten, were the six wonderful years Phyllis and I had been together in the Great State of Alaska, the small town pace of Yreka, California including the birth of our new daughter, Melody and the charm of Poway experiencing a different kind of world that I'm sorry to say we didn't find in the big cities of Sunny California.

Was I excited about the New Opportunity? **YES !!!!**

> *Looking back on our experiences in Southern California, I have never had one regret in making the decision to "Get Out Of Town" before we got deeply involved in the never ending rushing here and there trying to keep up with old friends and their lifestyles.*

> *We were in the Los Angeles Marketing area of Southern California from January to June 1968. I can't remember a day waking up with absolutely nothing to do except being with and enjoying our growing family.*

> *Moving to the "Great Northwest" with the opportunity to make a "Fresh Start" was something I just couldn't pass up.*

# Surprise... "Another Bottom Line"

Thanks for staying with me through the first 9 chapters.

This 1st book only covers 12 years of my life and I still have 38 more years to put on paper.

In the next 38 years, things really get exciting with "Getting A Hole in One" and winning a new car, Winning a Tiger Woods National contest and going to Las Vegas to meet Tiger, starting my own Sales & Marketing Company, and Costco Wholesale's entry into the Marketing World.

Thanks Again,

Billy P.

Cindy & Melody Sand Castle Masters!

Cindy at the beach

Huntington Beach House

Merry Christmas Tim!

Huntington Beach Easter time

Wolkramshausen
17. Maerz
5. Mai
ex decreto
25. Februar

# CHAPTER 11

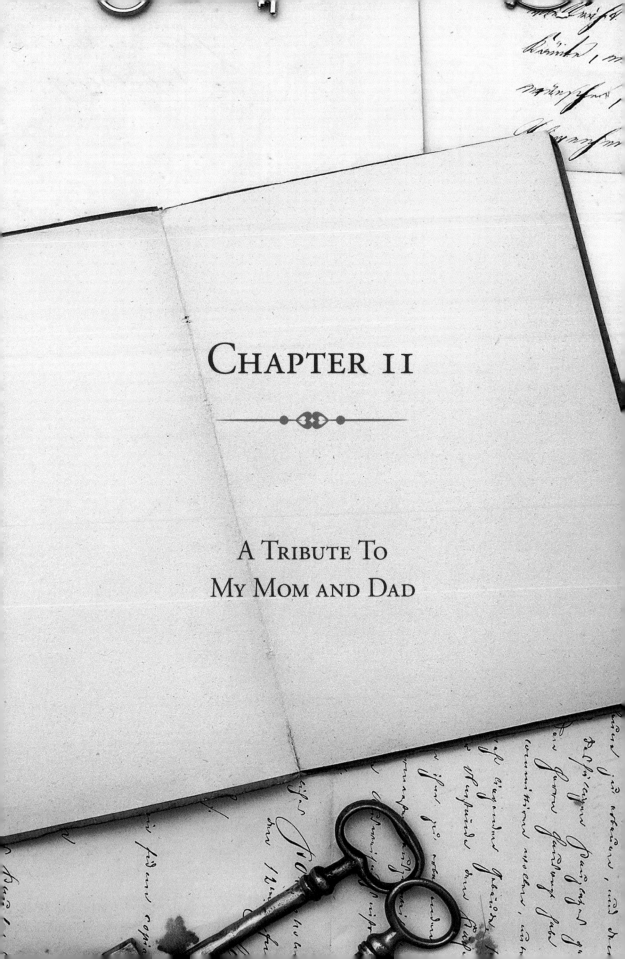

## A TRIBUTE TO
## MY MOM AND DAD

# My Mom, Wilma Matilda Perry
## (Never a Quitter)

*I* should have known from the day I was born, February 22nd, 1941, the Lord had put me in a very special place to be by my mom's side as we faced the trials and tribulations that were ahead in the years to come. It was George Washington's Birthday and I still can't tell a lie, most of the time.

As I write this "Love Letter" to my Mom, I'm at the ripe old age of 73 and honestly have a tough time remembering what happened last week, let alone 73 years ago.

Growing up was always a challenge for me in the early years. I was a great eater and was always taking extra cookies and putting them in my pocket. My mom never knew, nor did she? It seemed that we were always together doing kids stuff and baking cookies.

I had a problem that came up and it seemed to last for years. I had so many great dreams when I slept at night that I forgot to get up and go to the bathroom...and wet the bed. Mom was always there and never scolded me. I tried many different things to stop and nothing really helped until Mom found a cure in one of our magazines.

It was a rubber mat with aluminum foil strips attached to the mat. The mat was attached to an alarm system that would go off if it got wet. The noise would make me jump out of bed...and make me remember to go to the bathroom.

I was cured in less than a week. What a Joy!!!!

Our early years together seemed to fly by with me starting grammar school at Miles Avenue School and being dropped off each morning when my mom went to work at Sears & Roebucks as a catalogue sales person on the telephone. I use to call my mom at work from time to time and I remember the friends she worked with would say, Wilma, your daughter is on the phone.

With my Dad Charlie, working at the Sears & Roebuck warehouse and my older brother Chuck, who was in & out of the house from time to time, when he wasn't chasing girls in High School, my mom and I grew closer as the years went by.

Skipping ahead to my High School days, things changed dramatically in the early 60's when my Mom was diagnosed with Tuberculosis. I had no idea what that was and it was difficult for my dad to explain.

Mom was put in "Isolation" in her own bedroom and we could only talk with her from behind the clear plastic wall that had been set up. There was no hugging or touching and at times, it drove me crazy.

When I was finally told that the plastic wall was there so Mom wouldn't get any sicker and we wouldn't get sick either, I finally calmed down, cried and made it my job to take care of her every need, just like she did for me when I was a kid.

With the visits from doctors and nurses over the next several months, Mom began to improve rapidly and was free from her illness, and the feeling I had when we first touched has never gone away to this day.

It seemed that our lives were finally smoothing out and getting back to normal when my Mom & Dad returned from another doctor's appointment. I could see from my mom's tears that things weren't right and something was very wrong.

During the doctor's appointment which had included a complete physical the doctor had found several lumps in her left breast that required several tests that had to be done immediately in the hospital.

Exploratory Surgery was scheduled for the next day at Saint Francis Hospital in Lynnwood which was not far from our home.

I was about to learn, at a very early age, the devastation both Tuberculosis and Cancer could have on the human body and the possible results that would last forever. We were at the hospital for several hours which included the surgeon coming out to talk to my dad several times.

When all was said and done, the operation took her Left Breast, and found that the cancer had spread and then took all of the Lymph Nodes under her left arm just to make sure they got it all.

It has to be noted that way back in the 60's, Radiation and Chemotherapy had not been invented when all this was going on and the effects did last forever.

When my mom was in the hospital, there was a rule that no one under the age of 18 could visit patients on the upper floors who were recovering from major surgery. That included me at 16 and nothing could be done so I could see my Mom.

After much insistence, my dad got one of the Nuns to take me up the elevator to see my mom who would walk down the hall.

I'll never forget the emotion that I was filled with when the elevator door opened and there was my smiling mom standing there and I couldn't run up to her and fall into her arms and tell her that I loved her.

Have you ever had those feelings and couldn't do anything about them?

Mom finally came home for a long recovery and needed help every day. Dad stayed home for several weeks and then had to get back to work at Sears and Roebucks.

Having to go to school and leave mom home became a blur and I rushed home to be at her side and do anything she needed.

I guess that's when I started to do the things that were always done by her when she was well. I learned to make my bed, do the dishes, make a sandwich, with her supervision, do a load of laundry in the washing machine in the kitchen and even hang the clothes up on the clothes lines in the back yard.

There was no complaining for me, it was pure joy to be by her side and do everything I could do. I think I even learned to scrub the one toilet we had.

# ANOTHER MEMORY THAT WILL NEVER GO AWAY

om, It's impossible for me to imagine how you were able to celebrate your birthday on Thanksgiving Day 1961 when your son Chuck had just died in a car accident the night before...

I do remember that November 22nd morning when the police knocked on the front door. My mom peaked through the curtain to see who it was and there stood a Police officer with his hat in his hand.

I yelled for my dad to come to the door, which he did. We opened the door to the Police Officer and he asked if they were the parents of Charles Aquilla Perry Jr?

He asked if he could come in, which he did and then informed us that my brother Chuck had been killed in an automobile accident the night before in Huntington Beach.

What happened next is still a "Blur" with the crying and the tears that never seemed to end even now so many years later.

One thing I do remember and it's still crystal clear when I think about that day, is my Dad taking me aside, giving me a big hug with tears in his eyes and simply saying... "I'm glad it wasn't you".

I was just seventeen when this happened and I had no idea what I was experiencing except for my deep sorrow about my brother and how he died.

# My Dad,
# Charles Aquila Perry, Sr.
## (My Foundation)

It all started simple enough, just like most of the days for the past four or five years. As many of you know, I'm not a guy that sleeps-in. My normal waking time is 5am. This doesn't happen by chance or luck. It happens because around 3:30am, the newspaper deliver person with the bad muffler has come up the hill, stopped in front of my house, walked up the lawn and thrown my paper against the front door. Add to that, the sound of running water or rain and I have no choice!!!!

I use to think that the reason I got up, was to experience the total quietness of the hours before the activities of the world sneaks up on me and I'm committed to be "Off to the Races"...meeting the needs of my family and making the bucks that get us from one paycheck to the next.

The real reason I get up is because I'm doing, in my own way, just what my Dad, Charlie Perry did when I was growing up. Charlie had to retire early from his job at Sears Roebucks because he had a heart condition and there was very little that could be done in the 60's. He was told to go home and if he felt any pain in his chest, he was to take two nitro-glycerin tablets and rest. Charlie was not one that could just stop from what he was doing and rest. Sound familiar?

Since dad had been active in many Churches in the Southern California for years, he made the decision to start his own ministry that he could do while resting and staying home. We lived in a small two bedroom house, with a tiny bathroom that had two separate doors; a skinny kitchen where you could do all the cooking while standing in one position and it even had a washing machine to do your clothes laundry. The kitchen was always my favorite room because that's where all the chocolate chip cookies came from. If you made it through the kitchen by turning sideways, you could almost put the meal on the table in the breakfast nook which at one time was my bedroom with a very short bed. I should have spent more time in the nook for it was soon to disappear.

I can still remember my dad trying to figure out how his new ministry adventure was to get started when he had no place to set up all "His Stuff" while making no noise that would wake up the family. It didn't take him long to talk mom into letting him turn the nook into a recording studio for his ministry and he was off to the races on a new adventure. Sound familiar?

My dad wasn't a 5am riser but he did wake up to Dr. Kelfords ministry on the radio every morning before 6am. He spent time with the Lord in prayer, listening to different ministers on the radio, tape recording their messages on little cassette tapes and then sending them around the world to Christian missionaries for their encouragement.

What I do is really no different except that I'm using my computer to share my thoughts. In doing so, I can go out to the world using my eyes, my fingers and my memories to share what I have found and hopefully give others the encouragement they may need for their day that lies ahead.

Just because my dad Charlie was at home and "Medically Retired", didn't mean that he could just sit back and watch the world go by. With his Christian Ministry completed for the day, another brand new world was opening up and now he had time to explore all those things that he only dreamed about. He must have made some type of a "To Do List" several years before his ticker started giving him problems and he couldn't wait to get started.

One day, I asked my dad, where he got all his energy from? Sure enough, it was on his "To Do List" every day. He explained that every day from 12 noon to 12:30 was lunch time at work and he had a routine that he followed every day. There was a bench that he always sat on which measured 22 inches long and 12 inches wide. He always used his hands to show me what it looked like. His first 15 minutes of lunch was eating and the last 15 minutes he laid down on the bench and went immediately went to sleep. When he woke up...he started his 2nd day...every day. At the time, I thought that was amazing and it still is to this day.

While Charlie was working in the warehouse at Sears, there always seemed to be "Stuff" that was going to be thrown away and for some reason, Charlie always wanted to bring the "Stuff" home for some future project. We only had one car and it was an old Four-Door Lincoln Continental that was the size of a boat and just the right-size to haul lots of "Stuff" home.

I can still remember my mom getting phone calls in the afternoon from my Dad wanting us to pick him up by the trash dumpsters because there was some Great Stuff that he just had to have. I can remember my mom asking, "Where are you going to put all of this "Stuff". The answer was always the same; "In The Garage Of Course'.

I never saw his "To Do List"...but I know what had to be the number one project, "Find some place in the garage to put all this Great Stuff".

In 1970 Charlie & my mom Wilma Perry sold their home in the Los Angeles area and followed one of their dreams...to buy a double-wide mobile home in Hemet, California. It was about 100 miles from where we were living and it always seemed like an easy drive to see mom and dad.

Of course, it didn't take very long before they were members of the 1st Baptist Church of Hemet where many of their old friends were already members. The mobile home was perfect for them and they were enjoying the weather and all the long time friendships they had made over the years.

My dad didn't waste any time becoming an active member of their ministry team by tape recording everything that went on at church and their outreach into the community.

Hemet, California, is a small piece of paradise in the high desert on the way to Palm Springs that attracts thousands of visitors every year. The Annual Ramona Pagent is held in the Ramona Bowl Amphitheatre which is cut into the side of the mountain and seats over 5,000 people.

Of course, my Dad Charlie was there to experience the event and tape record all the music for the afternoon. He was sitting up at the top of the theatre in the back row with his friend of many years...

I can still imagine what must have been in his in his heart, just being there where the Lord was and recording everything that was going on.

I can see him now, with tears in his eyes and saying...

**"Wouldn't it be wonderful if the Lord came today"?**

**His Prayer was answered immediately and he was taken to heaven...**

The evening of July 31st, 1971 is sometimes still a blur. I received a phone call at 7:00pm from the hospital in Hemet, California and was told that my father, Charlie Perry had suffered a heart attack and I should get there "As Soon As Possible", and no other information was available.

Phyllis was bathing our two daughters, heard me crying and rushed in to see what had happened. When I told her the news, she quickly dressed the girls in their pajamas; we jumped in the car and were off to her mother's house so we could leave the girls there while we went to Hemet.

On a warm summer's day, the 90 mile trip was quick and enjoyable. The trip that evening seemed to go on forever especially when the end result was unknown. The entire trip, I tried to convince myself that he was ok and would apologize to us for having to come to Hemet and I could wrap my arms him and we would both have a good cry.

That wasn't to be and I never had a chance to say "Good Bye". And then again, maybe there wasn't a need.

As I've written this story, I realized that maybe, there wasn't a need to say goodbye because we would meet up "Every Afternoon" when I got ready to do what I always do in the afternoon... "Take a Nap".

It may sound crazy but it's true, there's only one difference. My dad's nap was 15 minutes and mine is 59 minutes when my alarm goes off.

# Thanks, Dad,

## FOR ALWAYS BEING WITH ME.

The tribute to my Mom and Dad.
Always loving.
Always caring.
Always faithful.
Always there to meet our many needs.

Thanks, Mom & Dad.

Wilma Perry 85th Birthday

Charlie Perry

..., ..., ...

... bestehen ...

..., ... ...emann,

Wolkramshausen

17. Maerz 183_

5. Mai ... schreiben: Fünfzig Thaler

... ... ... ... Hälfte, nach dem solche

... ... von Wermbschen Güter abgeschrieben

..., ex decreto vom 25. Februar 1834 ...

... zugeschrieben.

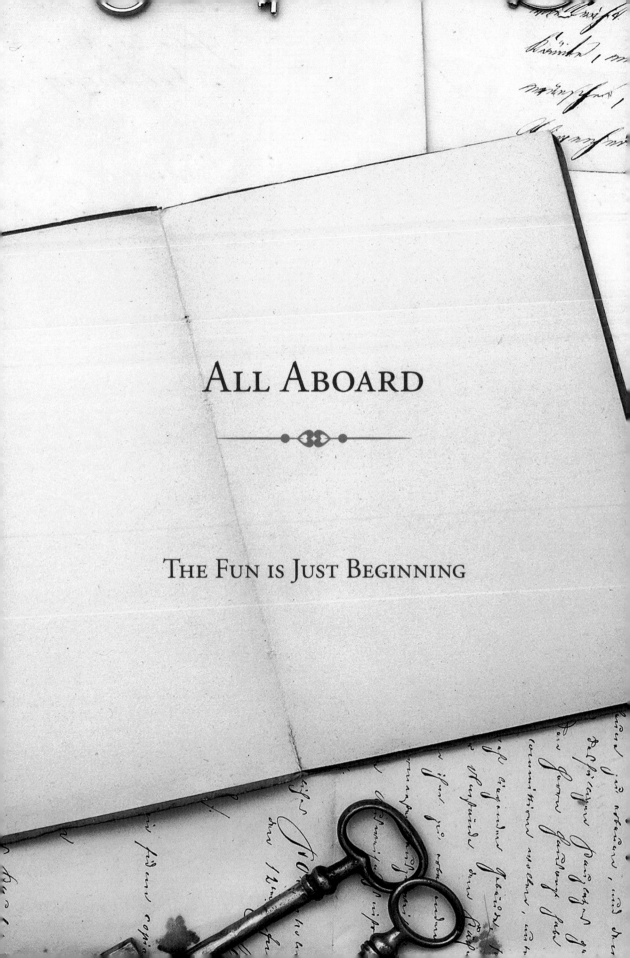

# All Aboard

## The Fun is Just Beginning

# ALL ABOARD

## THE FUN IS JUST BEGINNING

* Have you crossed the Atlantic Ocean on the Queen Elizabeth 2?

* Have you climbed the Eiffell Tower in Paris, France?

* Have you flown on the Concord Jet from London to New York?

* Have you experienced the thrill of making a "Hole in One" in golf and driven your new car home?

* Do you know Tiger Woods and have his picture on your piano?

\* Have you crossed the Alps in Switzerland and eaten fondue on the top of a mountain?

This is where the next book is going and I invite you to come along for a great adventure with us!!!

*With Much Love, Billy P.*